Praise for *Finding Our Way Home*

*"In my world, no one has more moral authority
than Diane Cirincione and Jerry Jampolsky.
Everything about them—from kindness, to their
marriage, and now to this highly important
book—inspires me to higher heights."*

— **Marianne Williamson**, the best-selling author of
A Return to Love and *The Age of Miracles*

*"If you could ever enjoy the pleasure of reading
a book to your soul in front of a fireplace, this
is the one I would recommend. Jerry and Diane
have given us a treasure chest full of wisdom and
warmth that makes you feel good all over, not
to mention spiritually centered once again."*

— **Caroline Myss**, the best-selling author of
Entering the Castle and *Anatomy of the Spirit*

ALSO BY THE AUTHORS

By Gerald G. Jampolsky, M.D., and Diane V. Cirincione, Ph.D.

A Mini Course for Life
Love Is the Answer: Creating Positive Relationships
Change Your Mind, Change Your Life
Simple Thoughts That Can Change Your Life
Wake-Up Calls
Me First and the Gimme Gimmes: A Story for Children of All Ages

By Gerald G. Jampolsky, M.D.

Love Is Letting Go of Fear
Teach Only Love: The Twelve Principles of Attitudinal Healing
Forgiveness: The Greatest Healer of All
Good-bye to Guilt: Releasing Fear Through Forgiveness
Out of Darkness into the Light: A Journey of Inner Healing
One Person Can Make a Difference:
Ordinary People Doing Extraordinary Things
Shortcuts to God: Finding Peace Quickly Through Practical Spirituality
"Listen to Me . . .": A Book for Women and Men
about Father-Son Relationships (with Lee L. Jampolsky, Ph.D.)

By Diane V. Cirincione, Ph.D.

Sounds of the Morning Sun

Audios, videos, DVDs, e-books, and
Internet-broadcast information are available at:
www.JerryJampolskyandDianeCirincione.com.

Please visit Hay House USA: **www.hayhouse.com**®
Hay House Australia: **www.hayhouse.com.au**
Hay House UK: **www.hayhouse.co.uk**
Hay House South Africa: **www.hayhouse.co.za**
Hay House India: **www.hayhouse.co.in**

Finding Our Way Home

Heartwarming Stories
That Ignite Our Spiritual Core

Gerald G. Jampolsky, M.D.
and
Diane V. Cirincione, Ph.D.

HAY HOUSE, INC.
Carlsbad, California • New York City
London • Sydney • Johannesburg
Vancouver • Hong Kong • New Delhi

Published and distributed in the United States by: Hay House, Inc.: www.hayhouse. com • **Published and distributed in Australia by:** Hay House Australia Pty. Ltd.: www. hayhouse.com.au • **Published and distributed in the United Kingdom by:** Hay House UK, Ltd.: www.hayhouse.co.uk • **Published and distributed in the Republic of South Africa by:** Hay House SA (Pty), Ltd.: www.hayhouse.co.za • **Distributed in Canada by:** Raincoast: www.raincoast.com • **Published in India by:** Hay House Publishers India: www.hayhouse.co.in

Editorial supervision: Jill Kramer • *Design:* Tricia Breidenthal

Library of Congress Cataloging-in-Publication Data

Jampolsky, Gerald G.
  Finding our way home : heartwarming stories that ignite our spiritual core / Gerald G. Jampolsky and Diane V. Cirincione.
    p. cm.
  ISBN-13: 978-1-4019-1793-7 (tradepaper) 1. Jampolsky, Gerald G. 2. Cirincione, Diane V. 3. Spiritual biography--United States. I. Cirincione, Diane V. II. Title.
  BL73.J36A3 2008
  299'.93--dc22
                                    2007031723

ISBN: 978-1-4019-1793-7

11 10 09 08   4 3 2 1
1st edition, April 2008

We have been blessed in life by having wonderful friends all over the world who love us and the work we are called to do. Two such couples are Ted and Vada Stanley and Larry and Joyce Stupski, and we dedicate this book to them with love and gratitude from our hearts to theirs.

The writing of these pages was specifically stimulated by Vada and Larry, who at different times seriously suggested that we pen a book solely consisting of stories about how people and events have helped shape our lives. Much to our delight, doing so has helped us further find our way Home.

Contents

$\mathscr{F}$oreword

Guides to Peace

Few authors have mastered the art of writing a spiritual story—which should be related with complete honesty, present a concept that is truly helpful, and invite change at the heart level.

Many published stories are a little preachy and just glib enough that their authenticity seems questionable. Consequently, they feed resistance rather than acceptance; and, sadly, even excellent spiritual advice may be dismissed by the reader.

Finding Our Way Home not only contains spiritual stories, it's virtually nothing *but* stories. This wouldn't be unusual in a work of fiction, but to present a bounty of real-life experiences of such insight and power is unparalleled. Furthermore, Jerry and Diane's accounts aren't slick or pat, nor do they moralize. As in the Hawaiian tradition of "talking story," they are intimate and friendly: It's as if two dear friends decide to share their most sacred experiences . . . and we feel deeply touched by the gesture.

Each entry contains a clearly defined mental step or guide. Taken together, these are like a course in wisdom, and the effect on us as readers is progressive and cumulative. Whether the subject is alcoholism, learning to laugh, self-loathing, healing the body, or changing our perceptions of death or the pace at which we think, there's a gentle mantra of key spiritual concepts throughout the book: *To forgive others is to forgive ourselves, to love is to know the*

Divine, to change our attitudes is to change our world, to still the mind is to have peace, and to extend happiness is to be reborn a child of God.

This book is as enjoyable as it is concrete and instructive. What better way to open our eyes than to be entertained while doing so! As I read these stories, I found myself savoring each one, like lying back on soft grass at night and cherishing the constellations above, one by one—the inevitable effect of which is to feel gently lifted up and pulled into the starry sky. To read *Finding Our Way Home* with the attention and affection it deserves is to feel oneness with the heaven that surrounds us all.

— **Hugh Prather,**
the best-selling author of *Notes to Myself*

$\mathscr{P}$reface

We're blessed to live in Hawaii half the year. Among the many wonderful things we've learned from residents of this precious land of cross-cultural diversity is the importance of "talking story."

In many ways, Hawaiians remind us that life is more than rushing about, business, and deadlines, as they take time to "talk story" in the course of their daily lives. Two or more people can recount a tale in a market, on the beach, while visiting with friends, or anywhere that fits. On the islands, even non-Hawaiians have learned to "talk story" when they get together.

Stories are one way in which hearts communicate. They're the sharing of one's own life and experience and serve as a means of connecting and joining with others. Not only are these heart connections a powerful vehicle for coming to know one other, but they can also facilitate profound learning in subtle ways. We believe that actual healing can occur when we learn from and share our heart stories with others.

These pages comprise some stories from *our* spiritual journey. Many are our personal accounts, while others are about people who have impacted our lives in profound ways. They chronicle the valleys we've fallen into, the mountains we've climbed, and some of the detours we've taken on our journey. We don't progress in a straight line . . . the stories often share the places we've called "home" as we've meandered through the years. Our lives continue to be works in progress as we do our best to remember that our true Home is a spiritual one, the Home of Love that we've never left and that always abides within us.

May these stories inspire you to further share your own heart with others, in the hopes that by doing so, we may all bring more light to an often-darkened world.

Introduction

Today many of us are caught up in the same fearful belief system, which tells us that we live in an unsafe world, there are enemies out there who need punishment, and our path in life is to put ourselves and our families first. Consequently, we worry about the future and try to get as much as we can and hold on to it, all the while believing that there is something external to us that will eventually bring us safety and everlasting happiness.

It's a belief system . . .

- . . . that accepts wars as inevitable and assumes that a permanent peace is impossible.

- . . . that doesn't regard others as our equals.

- . . . that thinks it's too bad so many people are starving or are in poverty, but there's nothing we can really do about it.

- . . . where many shrug their shoulders about the high rate of suicides; homicides; divorce; and physical, spiritual, and psychological abuse.

- . . . where we believe that holding on to grievances and unforgiving thoughts will get us what we really want.

However, more and more people—even though they may be financially and professionally successful—are discovering that money and accomplishments haven't brought them the happiness they thought would automatically result from "succeeding" in the world. And they still find themselves consumed by the fear that no matter how much they accumulate, the world is still a profoundly dangerous and frightening place to live.

Many of us eventually begin to question our purpose in life and feel that there has to be something greater than what we're experiencing. Sooner or later we ask ourselves: *What is the purpose of my life? Am I on the right road or simply plodding along in the same unhappy direction so many others have traveled? Where am I trying to go, and what am I trying to find?*

Why do so many of us feel lost, alone, anxious, fearful, and confused? Is it possible that we've simply taken the diverted road and followed our egos' signposts, which have blocked us from the awareness of our own spirituality?

It is our belief that although we may not be consciously aware of it, all of us are on a spiritual journey, even while pursuing other goals, and we're conflicted and unhappy because we've forgotten the essence of love that we are.

The two of us think of our pathway in life as a spiritual journey that's leading us to a consciousness composed of pure, unconditional, never-ending love. We're finding our way back to our Source, the Home of Love that we now believe we never really left.

Even though we're clear about our desire to be on a spiritual path, each day still provides challenges and circumstances that call to those parts of us that want to judge others or ourselves. What's different now is that we more quickly recognize when we're lost and the choice we have to return to the path of unconditional love. Once we remember that our purpose is service and helping others, as well as letting go of our judgments and grievances by practicing forgiveness, the path is easier, the direction clearer, and the destination of peace achievable.

This isn't a book about religion or theology; rather, it's a collection of stories that demonstrates the daily application of universal spiritual principles, something that we like to call *practical spirituality.* If the word *God* bothers you for any reason, you might want to substitute your own term—Infinite Intelligence, Universal Principle, Divine Source, Higher Power, or Natural Connection—or simply think of a Consciousness composed of pure, unconditional, never-ending Love.

Jerry: As a child in Long Beach, California, I grew up afraid of a punishing God's wrath, and at 16 I separated myself completely from the concept of a Higher Power when a close friend was killed in an automobile accident. I couldn't believe that there was a God Who would let that happen. With workaholism and then alcoholism as my home, I remained a militant atheist for decades . . . until I turned 50 and had what I would call a "spiritual awakening" to the oneness of humankind and the universality of a Presence in the world.

Because my childhood home was filled with so many insecurities and fears, I remember wondering what it would be like to live in one where there was no fighting or pain—where I could feel safe.

Looking back on the first half of my life as a researcher, professor, and child and adult psychiatrist, I can see that I took numerous detours that led me away from God and a spiritual life. Many of these side roads, however, are what have led me to where I am today.

Diane: I grew up in the Bronx and on Long Island in New York. I loved my family and felt loved by them. However, my father had an unpredictable and volatile temper, and conflicts would frequently end in domestic violence. I was often fearful and somewhat insecure, and I tried unsuccessfully to be the family peacemaker. I too used to wonder what it would be like to live in a place where there was only love and peace and where no one would ever dream of hurting another person.

As I grew older, workaholism was the way I detoured from finding my way home. It served as an escape mechanism that kept me too busy to deal with unresolved issues from my childhood. For example, there was a time when I owned three businesses at once, and along with my partner, I put in 12- to 14-hour days, seven days a week, for many years. Predictably, the unresolved issues didn't go away by burying them in work. Instead, they continued to surface in relationships, and it took years to identify and ultimately work through them. Getting my master's and Ph.D. in clinical psychology with a specialization in domestic violence helped me better understand these family dynamics, although in the end I still had to do the personal-growth work myself.

In contrast to Jerry, I grew up feeling close to God but periodically separated myself through my fears.

We both believe that while our lives have been quite different, we were each searching for that peaceful place inside where, through forgiveness, there is finally only love . . . which at first seemed like a dream figment of our childhood imaginations. This book is about part of our journey together and our learning process in finding that the peaceful home we were both seeking isn't something external, but instead lies within each of us.

We met in 1981, and two and a half years later we began traveling around the world together in response to requests to lecture and give workshops on the diverse applications of Attitudinal Healing*—which is the realization that ultimately it's not other people or events from our personal histories that are still making us upset, but rather our thoughts, attitudes, and judgments that are causing us distress. We can't change the past, but by using

---

* If you're not familiar with Attitudinal Healing, please go to the Appendix of this book to find more information about the International Centers for Attitudinal Healing throughout the world, or visit the Website: **www.attitudinalhealing.org**.

the Principles of Attitudinal Healing, we can heal our minds and hearts in the present, move out of the victim role, maximize our choices in life, and choose peace over conflict and love over fear.

In 1990, we married. From the beginning, it has been clear to us that our meeting wasn't an accident . . . that we were spiritual partners and teachers for each other. By making peace of mind our only goal, we try to do our best to step aside and let God lead the way as we reach for harmony and integrity in all that we think, say, and do. We're not always there, but we continue to journey together in that direction.

Our path has been blessed by meeting people of all ages, from diverse cultures and walks of life—a few of whom are mentioned in these pages. They turned out to be our teachers of life, love, and forgiveness. By touching our hearts in some unique way, they've helped us find our way home. We're grateful to be able to share our stories and theirs, and hope that doing so will inspire you to embrace all *your* stories as signposts that have also shown you a way home.

— **Jerry Jampolsky, M.D.**, and
Diane Cirincione, Ph.D.

How We Met

— Jerry

My relationship with Diane began many months before we met in person. At the time, she had left the corporate world and was deeply involved in helping run three companies, working long hours from her offices—which, like mine, were located in Tiburon, California.

Two years prior to our meeting, she'd had a profoundly spiritual experience of being temporarily blinded by the early-morning sun, which initiated a flow of thoughts that she began to put onto paper. In February of 1981, Diane received a complex message to give something to the person who worked with the children who were dying. Intuitively, she knew that the "something" was her writing. She concluded that since she only had one piece on death, that's what she should present to the man who had recently started an innovative center working with children who were terminally ill. She thought that it might be helpful.

Early the following Sunday morning, Diane found my address in the phone book, placed her essay in an envelope with a brief note, and put it in my mailbox. She had no guidance to sign her name and left it without a signature. About two hours later, an old friend called, offering her an invitation to The Continuum Event in San Francisco, a series of lectures on the subject of death and dying and life after death. The friend was going to see Dr. Kenneth

Pelletier, someone whose work Diane had read and admired, so she accepted.

Even though I'd gotten my mail on Saturday afternoon, something inside moved me to check it again on Sunday morning. Much to my surprise, I found a letter that someone had left there. The person had chosen not to sign it, indicating that no response was necessary, which I thought was quite unusual.

The writing was beautiful and touched me deeply, and since it concerned death and dying, I put the letter in my coat pocket and proceeded to drive to San Francisco, where I was scheduled to lecture on that very subject. In the middle of the talk, I decided to read the letter aloud, and it was very well received. I didn't know that the person who had written it was in the audience. Diane wasn't aware that I would be on the panel, and since she had no guidance to introduce herself, she didn't, and left after the lecture.

Many months later, she shared that while sitting in the audience that day, she had asked quietly inside, *What does this mean that I wound up here today and this man is reading my words?* The answer she clearly got was that what she'd written had value to others besides herself.

Almost six months passed before Diane received another message, which was to bring me all of her writings. She ignored the guidance . . . then, on August 20, 1981, she was driving to her office at 6:30 in the morning when her car suddenly died on Main Street, right in front of the alley entrance to the Center for Attitudinal Healing. Diane felt a strong inclination not to attempt to restart it, but to instead get out and ignore her inner voice no longer. Not sure where to go, she walked toward the dock and found herself in front of a blue door with a rainbow painted across it, which she proceeded to knock on. She later told me that her mind felt split at that moment as one part of her was judging her actions as completely insane while the other just "knew" they were right.

When I opened the door, we both experienced a jolt. Months later, Diane told me that at the moment I opened the door, very bright light filled the air with a golden mist. Simultaneously, most sound ceased for her, and she could barely hear me when I asked what she wanted.

An inner voice guided her words as she replied, "There's this writing I'm supposed to share with you."

Since I was talking with someone in my office, I asked her to come back in an hour when I had a break. When she returned, we spent about 20 minutes together, during which my heart skipped some beats. It was 7:45 A.M., and Diane, who had been on her way to her office to do some cleanup work, was dressed in grubby clothes, with her hair pulled back in a ponytail. Yet there was a balance of outer and inner beauty and a gentleness that was beyond anything I'd previously experienced. There was something breathtaking about the experience: an amazing sensation of an ancient familiarity—a feeling that we had met at another time, in another place. It was like two souls coming together who had known each other many times before. The office seemed to light up with the energy between us.

This was a difficult and chaotic period in my life. The voice of my ego was incessant, well aware that the fence I'd carefully built around my heart had come down for a moment. My ego wanted me to not only repair it, but to build it even higher, and it even resorted to using spirituality as a way of keeping me in bondage.

My conversation with myself went something like this: *You're finally on a spiritual pathway. The last thing you need is a new "special relationship" with a beautiful woman who's more than 20 years your junior. Stop your fantasies. If this relationship becomes romantic, it will lead you away from your purpose. Don't add more obstacles.*

When I tried to argue, my ego cut in: *How many times do I have to tell you that you'll be a failure with women no matter what? Close relationships have always gone wrong, and they always will. You'll just end up getting hurt and hurting her. She came to you for help with her writing, not to have a personal relationship. Forget about your loneliness—that's your destiny. Be objective and helpful, but don't make any more appointments to see her.*

Inside, another little voice said that Diane was truly a gift and had come into my life to teach me that the way Home to God was allowing a close *personal* relationship to become a *holy* one. All this inner chatter made me feel as if I were losing my sanity. But I did make another appointment with Diane, and the next time we got together, I tried to be objective and keep an emotional distance, while inside I was petrified with fear. I wanted so much to do the right thing and not fall into pain and misery again. We continued to meet in my office.

Some months later, I finally mustered the courage to invite Diane to lunch. I didn't realize what a powerful teacher she was going to be for me in the years ahead, and the first lesson started that very day. When I automatically went to pick up the tab, she gently asked what I was doing. I told her that I was going to pay the bill. She inquired why I was going to pay *her* bill. I said that I assumed I always paid it. She then suggested that our friendship would go a lot further and have a much better chance of success if she took her bill and I took my assumptions, and we could proceed from there.

Throughout the more than 25 years that have followed, we've continued to help each other look at *all* of our assumptions, and we've both grown enormously. Diane is still my treasured teacher, my best friend, my spouse, and my spiritual partner.

Because our egos are preoccupied with past mistakes,
they counsel us to never take risks and to never trust our
own hearts. But an unexpected meeting can prove to be life
changing and even lead us to find our spiritual soul mate.
When in doubt, we must listen to our hearts.

A Change in Course

— Diane

Two years after Jerry and I met, I reluctantly gave him permission to share some of my writings—which he loved to use as meditations—in his talks and workshops. I did so only on the condition that he not mention my name. I had absolutely no interest in my private reflections being made public and had an actual aversion to ever being in public life myself.

Whenever Jerry would hint at my sharing something at a talk or lecture, I always refused. I thought he was doing this not because he really wanted my input, but simply to keep me close to him. I had no conception that there was anything beneficial that I could say to anyone in public.

Jerry was scheduled to lecture in Santa Rosa, California, about one hour north of San Francisco. He was completely healthy except for one thing: The day before, he had woken up with absolutely no voice, not even a whisper. Since more than 500 people were signed up to attend, the staff at the Center for Attitudinal Healing agreed to accompany him onstage and be his "voice" for the evening.

Jerry asked me to drive him to the event, which I did. En route, the two of us stopped to get something to eat, and by mouthing the words, he silently inquired if, since he couldn't read my meditations as he usually did at the beginning and end of his talk, I would consider doing so myself.

"Absolutely *not!*" I replied so loudly that the couple at the next table actually turned around and stared at me. A bit agitated by the request, I returned to my meal.

A few moments passed, and Jerry tapped my arm to get my attention so I could read his lips. Still a bit irritated, I looked up at him. With no sound, he mouthed, "I heard what you said, but I'm just wondering if you prayed on the request before you answered." We'd learned over the years to always ask for guidance before making decisions.

I replied, "No, I didn't."

He asked if I would be willing to do so right now, before I made a final decision. Begrudgingly, I agreed.

When I asked internally if I should do what he asked, I got an unmistakable *Yes.* I hesitated and then told him my answer, quickly followed by: "If I find out that you're faking this laryngitis just to get me to do this, I'm going to kill you!" He laughed inaudibly, and his eyes twinkled the way they often do.

We continued on to the event, and as I read my writings and did the meditations, my whole consciousness altered. I could see light and soft colors filtered through a mist coming from the audience, as if to "read" their energies. Internally, I felt connected to the Source and the Divine Mother—something I'd never come this close to experiencing before. I felt more "at home" doing this than I'd previously felt in all of my (then) 36 years.

Without needing to express it, Jerry and I both knew what had occurred: It was a Divine calling to change the course of my life, go in the direction of the Light, and help me find my way Home. What a gift to be journeying there together!

It's easy to remain on the automatic pilot of the ego voice, which is based in fear, when it comes to making decisions. When we still our minds and look to our hearts for answers, what comes back is based on love and connection. The inner peace we feel gives us the assurance that we're on the right track.

The Golden Gate Bridge

— Jerry

Throughout my life, the ability of human beings to recover from serious problems has astonished me. It's almost as if we have a special "rubber" gene that allows us to bounce back from even the most difficult circumstances. In times when I'm down, I look to individuals who have demonstrated this ability as my teachers. I've been privileged to know some of these people in my role as a therapist. Remembering their resiliency always helps me reawaken my own innate strength and courage.

Before I was involved in Attitudinal Healing, I had a 35-year-old single woman as a client who was depressed and feared that she'd commit suicide by jumping off the Golden Gate Bridge. I saw her in psychotherapy for about six months, and in that time she improved dramatically. Once the therapy was concluded, our paths didn't cross again.

About 20 years later, Diane and I were driving from Marin County to the airport in San Francisco before daybreak. As I handed our toll to the attendant at the Golden Gate Bridge, she looked at me, broke out in an enormous smile, and said, "Dr. Jampolsky, do you remember me? I was your patient who was afraid she was going to commit suicide by jumping off the Golden Gate Bridge—and just look at me now!" We exchanged greetings, but because there was a lot of traffic, I had to move on and couldn't talk further.

For the next several years, it was our good fortune to meet at the tollbooth and know how important we were to each other.

There's no limit to inner healing. We can always choose to climb the very mountain that has previously terrified us. Each of us has the strength to face any type of adversity, no matter how old or persistent.

Poppy Seeds

— Diane

Jerry loves a good bagel with poppy seeds—hundreds of poppy seeds. While consuming one, he often leaves a trail of seeds en route from the kitchen to his study. I know that when he sees them on the floor, he *tries* to pick them up . . . but Jerry's standard of "picking them up" is, unfortunately, very different from mine.

I frequently find myself cleaning up poppy seeds with a wet hand towel upon entering our white-floored kitchen whenever they're inadvertently left behind. I do so easily and generally, without much thought.

One day I remember feeling particularly grumpy about something unrelated as I went downstairs and entered the kitchen. I looked down and saw poppy seeds scattered all around, and my "grumpy" level increased. After grabbing and moistening the hand towel a little bit more robustly than I usually do, I began to bend down to pick up the seeds. I distinctly remember having the thought: *Just once, I would like to come into the kitchen and not find these poppy seeds!* My very next thought was: *What if the floor never had any more poppy seeds on it?* The answer bolted into my mind like a flash of lightning: *It would mean that there would never be any more Jerry!*

Tears flooded my eyes as I stood up. I gazed down at those poppy seeds, and they looked so good to me. I turned around, rushed into Jerry's study, and threw my arms around him, kissing him while I cried tears of joy.

Now, regardless of what I find on the kitchen floor, no matter how many seeds I may mop up, I'm peaceful inside. Whenever I see those poppy seeds, they fill me with love and gratitude; and on some days I deliberately leave them and my old compulsive behavior behind as I smile, turn, and walk away.

*Any two people will have dissimilar ways of doing things,
and if we love someone, we embrace those differences. But isn't it
amazing how when we're upset, our egos grab hold of small things
and turn them into a big deal? It never ceases to amaze us that
one seemingly insignificant incident can transform an
old behavior and the way we are in our world.*

What Was Once Wrong Made Right

— Diane

Growing up, I had an older sister and brother, Kathryn and Andrew. When I was about ten, we moved from the Bronx to a little country town on Long Island called Lake Ronkonkoma. Each day, accompanied by our faithful dog, Duchess, we walked down the block to attend St. Joseph's Grammar School.

Kathryn was smart, worked very hard, and did extremely well in school. Andrew was just as smart and worked as hard, but did poorly. It would be decades before we discovered that my brother had a form of dyslexia that caused him to perceive each word on a page as floating, which required him to strain his eyes to settle it down. While he reads quite well today, throughout his younger years it was a traumatic experience, since no one in those days was trained to diagnose or treat dyslexia.

Most of the Catholic nuns who taught us were dedicated teachers and well intentioned. Since we were seated each semester according to our grade average in class, Andrew and some of the other students were always assigned the last seats of the back row. This strict code of ranking was shaming for most of us, particularly the boys and girls who had personal challenges that others were unaware of.

The nuns were often particularly harsh to those in the last row—especially the sixth-grade teacher, Sister Evidia, who had to deal with 11- to 13-year-old boys two heads taller than she. I remember her as an extremely heavy middle-aged woman with exceptionally thick glasses. Some of her students had been retained a grade or two for undiagnosed dyslexia, and these kids were generally labeled "poorly motivated." (Not being able to see, read, or comprehend as most others do will definitely dampen your motivation!) The painful and unjust psychological and social scars can remain for a lifetime.

Years passed, and we all moved away from our little town to the far corners of the country. The three of us siblings made our way in the world, succeeding equally at life, love, family, and careers. Four decades would pass before justice would have its due and a well-meaning wrong would be made right.

Although Jerry and I reside in both Northern California and Hawaii, visits to the beautiful home of Andrew and his wife, Karen, in East Quogue on Long Island's Great South Bay are frequent and always wonderful. On one such trip a few years ago, Andrew asked if I wanted to take a drive back to the old neighborhood. I told him that I would like to very much, but had to admit that I was quite surprised *he* wanted to go. We hopped in his car and off we went to "The Lake," about an hour away.

So much had changed that I was somewhat disoriented. We drove by our old house, and Andrew suggested that we visit our old grammar school, which was down the block. Again, I expressed surprise that he would even consider returning, since many of his memories were so painful. He seemed determined to see it, so we drove over and turned into the driveway.

We entered the school yard, and memories flooded back as Andrew made another suggestion that absolutely shocked me: "Let's go over to the convent where the nuns live and see who's there."

I said, "Andrew, I'm certain that all the nuns we knew have transferred elsewhere and retired or are more than likely dead. It's been almost 50 years, and surely no one would know us there."

He insisted that we needed to go, which was extremely uncharacteristic of him. However, knowing how intuitive he's always been, I followed his lead, got out of the car, and approached the little two-story house in the middle of the playground.

As we walked toward the door, we noticed that in the small enclosed garden to the left of the building was someone with her back to us dressed in a black habit. Andrew said, "Let's see who that is." We walked up behind the person, and as she turned around, my heart literally skipped a beat. It couldn't be, but it was: Sister Evidia, now some 90-plus years of age.

Startled, she asked who was there, saying that her eyes had failed her long ago. I stuttered a bit but finally said, "Sister Evidia, I don't know if you remember me—I'm Diane Cirincione, Tom and Phyllis's daughter."

Her face lit up like a child's, and she replied, "Praise God, Diane, of course I remember you. Tell me, please, how is your brother, Andrew?"

I was taken aback once again because she didn't ask about my parents, both of whom she'd known quite well. I replied, "Well, Sister, he's very well, and in fact he's right here with me, standing just to your left."

Tears welling up in her eyes, she swung around, reached out her hands, and said, "Andrew, Andrew, is that you?"

I looked quickly at his face, which once again was filled with the childhood nervousness and lack of assurance that I remembered all too well. When he spoke, I could hardly hold back the tears as he began to apologize to her: "Sister, I am so sorry I gave you a bad time."

She immediately stopped him, and taking his hands, said, "No, Andrew, no. It is *I* who must apologize to you and thank God I've lived long enough to do so. I don't live here anymore and was just visiting this one week. It's a miracle that you're here. Andrew, we just didn't know in those years what we know today about the different ways children learn. I spent so much time scolding kids like you who were acting out. I also missed the calls for help from the very silent ones who had even more problems. Andrew, please forgive me for all the wrongs I've done to you."

My brother's eyes were now filled with tears as he said, "Sister, there's nothing to forgive. We all did the very best we could with what we had to cope with then. I always knew that you cared about us. Thank you, Sister—thank you."

We visited a while longer before we embraced Sister Evidia, said our good-byes, and quietly left her still standing in the garden as we slowly departed. Driving back home, we sat in stunned yet contented silence.

Clearly, this was beyond chance or coincidence, and finally we spoke with gratitude for the healing of a painful chapter in life, recognizing it as a tremendous blessing. A few months later, we heard that at the end of a long life of service, Sister Evidia had died peacefully in her sleep.

What often seems like chance in our lives is truly more
than just that. Another way of looking at a coincidence is to
see it as a miracle in which God wishes to remain anonymous.

The Fishing Pole

— Jerry

In 1957, I had a ten-year-old patient whom I'll fictitiously call Jeffrey Jones. I saw Jeffrey and his mom separately for psychotherapy.

My office in Tiburon in Northern California was located on pilings out on the water. I often fished with the kids I saw in my practice, because I felt children were typically more relaxed and open to talking in this context. On his birthday, I gave Jeffrey a small fishing pole and never really thought about the gift again.

Many years later, Diane wrote a beautiful book and wanted to find an illustrator who would paint an original picture for the cover. She investigated and discovered that one of the best illustrators in the country, Jeffrey Jones, happened to live fairly close to us in the Bay Area.

Although I didn't think it could possibly be the same Jeffrey Jones I'd known 33 years before, I was curious enough about the coincidence to ask Diane if I could accompany her to the meeting. The artist's studio was located in his home . . . and lo and behold, it was the same Jeffrey Jones! Meeting him again and being able to share my enthusiasm for his success was a wonderful experience. He insisted that he wanted to do the cover of Diane's book as a gift to us. We spent about two hours visiting with Jeffrey, his wife, and his two children.

Just as we were leaving, Jeffrey said that he wanted to show me something, and then disappeared for a few moments. When he returned, he was holding the little fishing pole I'd given him all those many years ago. Without saying a word, he reached out and handed me the small rod. In the room's silence were the unspoken words: *This meant a lot to me—enough for me to keep it all these years.* Tears came to my eyes as I recognized how important our relationship had been to him.

Jeffrey was a teacher coming back into my life to remind me of the significance of what I'd thought was merely a small act of kindness.

*It's easy to underestimate the impact that a single
gesture of love can have on another person's life.
Giving and receiving truly are one and the same.*

*During one of several meetings we had with her,
Mother Teresa stated that there's no such thing as a
"small" or a "big" act of love. <u>All</u> acts of love, she said,
are the same, and they aren't measurable, because
they come from the purity of our hearts.*

$\mathcal{F}$ear as a Way of Life

— Jerry

Fear, and how we deal with it, is one of the most important challenges in life; and today the level of this harmful emotion in the world has increased dramatically. Although individuals may focus their fear differently—dwelling on terrorism, the economy, being alone, losing jobs, or death; or just harboring a general dread that encompasses many areas—as a people, we are afraid. With the advent of 24-hour news programs, we can tap into an endless stream of pessimism and listen to conflicting arguments about what should be done, which leaves most of us confused and even more frightened. So pervasive is this mind-set that unless we're aware of the alternative, we live in a continual state of alarm, of which many of us are unaware. To compensate, we fill our lives with numerous activities, thereby overriding our sensitivity to the anxiety.

Because I spent so much of my life being afraid, I know what this state of mind does to an individual. As a child, I was terrified of high places, the ocean, the "bogeyman," meeting new people, school, and just about anything you could name. I carried this emotion into my adulthood, trying to camouflage it as much as possible, under the assumption that if it didn't show, it didn't matter.

Because I believe that we teach what we want to learn, my first book, *Love Is Letting Go of Fear,* was really my own inner therapy.

The fact that it also helped millions of people from diverse cultures made me realize that my house of fear was actually very crowded. I wasn't alone in needing another way to look at the world and a different method for making decisions. It's also no accident that my work in Attitudinal Healing dealt with children and adults who were facing the fear of death.

All of us are works in progress, but Diane and I have decided to make our decisions based on love instead of fear as often as we possibly can. But what does this mean? Most spiritual truths are actually quite simple, and so is this one. Fear comes from the ego, which isn't our real identity. Egos feel alone because they're cut off from their original Source and from each other. When we experience our oneness with our Source, we also feel it with each other, and our decisions reflect that.

Without exception, the most common underlying fear in every single problem we have is that of separation from someone or something. Think about any fear you have—whether it relates to your family, job, organization, or country. Then ask yourself, *What—or whom—am I afraid of being separated from?* It may be someone's love, a person whose death is impending, or socioeconomic concerns involving money or work. Inherent in each one is the fear of separation or loss. Just recognizing this allows you to make conscious choices out of love rather than unconscious ones out of fear.

Fear separates us—from each other and from our Source. Isn't it time to move away from the endless stream of conflicted thoughts and toward the only answer that can transform not only our individual lives, but also the world? Perhaps rather than another ideology, what we need is a spiritual transformation that encompasses everyone and everything. For this to happen, we must turn from fear to love.

Fear Is Never the Answer

— Jerry and Diane

In 1988, we were at the University of California, Santa Barbara, to film the Dalai Lama for a nationwide television special, *Children as Teachers of Peace*. This was also the name of our international 1980s project in which we took children to Russia, China, and Central America to meet with heads of state and others in positions to affect many lives.

We'd selected 30 boys and girls to have a dialogue with His Holiness, who was seated under a tree, with a child sitting on either side of him. The rest of us formed a semicircle facing him.

Just before the cameras started rolling, a woman came rushing up to inform us that the six-year-old girl to the right of His Holiness was very hyperactive and would be all over the place in only a few minutes. For the sake of the film, she advised us to "replace this girl immediately or she'll ruin the shot." After thanking her for the information, we decided to go behind a large tree to pray about what to do.

We both received the same clear answer: not to act from fear, but rather to leave the little girl where she was and proceed just as we'd planned.

About five minutes after the filming began, the child became drowsy and gradually lowered her head onto His Holiness's lap. He gently stroked her hair as she slept through the rest of the filming, which proceeded quite smoothly. When we'd finished, she woke, stood up, and later told the Dalai Lama that she was really glad he came to Santa Barbara that day.

To respond from fear simply invites it into the situation. A fearful state of mind tends to draw fear-filled experiences to it. We can choose to turn within and ask with humility, stillness, and openness, <u>What is it that I need to know?</u>

$\mathcal{E}$xperiencing Bernadette

— Diane

Sometimes as children we're lucky to know someone our own age who's far more evolved than their years should merit (I don't mean in a way that creates separation or jealousy, but rather in a way that inspires and illuminates the possibilities for our own potential). Growing up, my friends and I had such a person in Bernadette Schenone.

Although a few of us knew her when she was younger, most of us first met Bernadette at 14 when we entered Seton Hall High School in the small town of Patchogue, on the south shore of Long Island. The school drew its students from a 60-mile radius that included dozens of tiny communities, so we rarely knew how poor or rich anyone else was because we lived far away from each other and wore uniforms. Somehow it all worked beautifully.

Bernadette had a quiet, friendly way about her and was always sensitive to the feelings and ideas of others. While she was very popular and certainly had close friends, she wasn't in a clique. Many girls sought her out, and she always had time for everyone. I can now see that there was a deeply spiritual quality about Bernadette . . . a calmness in her presence that drew people to her.

As we began our senior year, only a few of her friends knew how sick Bernadette was, and that was only because one of their mothers had been her oncology nurse when she was in the hospital.

21

The rest of us initially thought that although she had some challenges, she would soon be fine and back at school.

When you're young, things that haven't yet been a part of your reality tend not to cross your mind. The possibility of Bernadette dying was so beyond my frame of reference that I never considered it. Coming from a large Italian family, I was familiar with death. I wasn't uncomfortable with it, because I'd experienced it as a natural part of life for those who were old and ready to go. But like so many things we think we understand, death isn't part of our expectations when it's out of context.

Bernadette's loving mother invited about a dozen of her close friends to visit their home in early April after she'd spent a winter's absence from school. Bedridden, thin, and weak though she was, her inner light shone as beautifully as ever. As I look back on that day, I can see that I was probably the only girl who didn't know that Bernadette was dying and this was our final good-bye.

I remember looking at the spots on her legs and commenting on them in such a way that it was obvious I believed that someday they'd be gone. The room grew silent, and I felt an awkwardness come over me. In the nervous tone of an insecure teenage girl, I asked, "Bernadette, when *are* you coming back to school?"

At that point one of my classmates raised her eyebrows, made a sound, and put her hand over her face as if to say, *Oh my God, I can't believe she asked that!* There was a pause, and then Bernadette smiled at me with all the love in her heart, as if to protect and console me in this uncomfortable moment. She was that kind of person.

The following day in the senior girls' locker room, my friend Maureen Hawkins took me aside and gently said, "Diane, Bernadette isn't coming back to school." I'll remember that moment for the rest of my life because it all suddenly made sense. I don't think I expressed it then, but I was so grateful to Maureen for helping me understand—everyone else had just assumed that I knew.

The life work that Jerry and I have chosen includes many direct confrontations with death, of both the young and old. I've learned how our fears can make us deny what's right in front of us, and I understand the defense mechanisms that we often employ to protect us in the face of something too painful to grasp. But I learned this first from Bernadette, and I'll always be thankful for the lessons she taught me, both in her life and in her death.

Death is a certainty for all of us, but it need not be a terrifying vision that we push away with our defenses and fears. Our true reality is spiritual—that which is real within each of us is also eternal and can't be extinguished.

A Child's Vision of Death

— Jerry

At the International Center for Attitudinal Healing in Sausalito, California, one of our principles is that each individual is equally a teacher and a student to everyone else. This means that a small child can be as powerful an instructor as an adult with the highest credentials. When we accept whomever we're with as our teacher regardless of their behavior, we see—and act quite differently in—the world.

In 1977, when the Center was located in Tiburon, California, one of the first children to die was Greg Harrison. He was 11 years old; and after numerous rounds of chemotherapy, he, his parents, and his physician decided to stop his treatments.

In the Center's group for children with life-threatening illnesses, one of the other boys asked Greg, "What's it like to know that you're going to be dead in a few weeks?"

I was the facilitator of the group that night and was shocked at the directness of this question. As I tried to think of what to say to take Greg off of the hot seat, he calmly replied, "I think that when you die, you just lay aside your body, which was never real in the first place. Then you go to heaven and become one with all souls. And sometimes you come back to Earth and act as a guardian angel to someone."

Like so many children with potentially fatal diseases who have come to our Center, Greg was wise beyond his years. We think of these kids as spiritual teachers in small bodies who show us another way of looking at life and death. Greg's effect on me has been profound, and there isn't the slightest question in my mind that he has been, and continues to be, *my* guardian angel.

Our bodies are just the houses we live in while we're on Earth. Our real identity is spiritual and eternal. The essence of our being is Love.

ℒetting Go
of a Grievance

— Jerry

In 1975, I was seeing a 16-year-old high school student in my psychotherapy practice. She was headstrong and belligerent and was a serious problem for both her divorced mother and her school. I saw her weekly for six months, and over that period her behavior improved dramatically. At that point, she and her mom moved to another state.

The girl's father, who lived in Missouri, had agreed to cover the cost of her treatment, but in its six-month duration he didn't pay a single bill. I made a few phone calls to him, and he always said, "I'll send you a check next week." But none ever arrived. Needless to say, I found myself getting angry with this man. Since he was the CEO of a large company, I knew that he could easily afford my fee.

I was proud of the progress his daughter had made in therapy, but my anger about not being paid caused me to consider turning the bill over to a collection agency, something I'd never previously done. Despite the fact that my feelings were "justified," they weren't bringing me peace of mind. During my morning meditation, I received guidance to do something that would release both him and me from this unhappy situation.

I called the man and shared with him my truth—specifically, that I had been angry with him for not paying any of his daughter's bills. I wanted him to know that I'd changed my perception, had forgiven myself for my anger, and was now also at peace with him. I added that I didn't know why he hadn't paid any of the bills—I didn't need to know—and that it was okay if he never paid them, because I wasn't going to send him any more. I wished him well, saying that my purpose in calling was to release both of us from further friction or anxiety, and I was very peaceful with this decision. After a long silence, he said, "Thank you for your call," and that was the end of our conversation.

The process of both forgiving him for not paying and myself for my anger created an immediate sense of tranquility at a level I'd never previously experienced. My mind felt calm, free, and whole.

I had no expectation of ever hearing from the man again, so imagine my surprise when a week later a check for six months of therapy arrived in the mail. Along with his payment was a note thanking me for the call and saying how much our conversation had meant to him. While the money was a nice and unexpected outcome, I was grateful that my peace of mind had come *before* the check and wasn't dependent upon it.

There are two essential lessons forgiveness teaches us:
(1) Inner peace is more important than "justified" anger
or any other ego emotion that separates us from each other,
and (2) our peace doesn't depend on the outcome of the
situation we find ourselves in—rather, it depends on
whether we forgive. The power of forgiveness sets us
free under all circumstances and in every way.

Opening My Heart

— Diane

Jerry and I were at the University of California, Santa Barbara, to film a documentary we were creating about children searching for peace amid the nuclear threat and strained Soviet-American relations in the mid-1980s. Kids from diverse walks of life were gathered on the lawn of the chancellor's home, along with His Holiness the 14th Dalai Lama. The dialogue was filmed as part of an effort to find the way home to a peaceful world.

After the filming was complete and everyone was milling around and beginning to say good-bye, His Holiness quietly walked across the lawn and stood in front of me. Instead of being startled, as I might have envisioned, I felt a gentle warmth surrounding both of us. He took my hands in his, drew me inches away from his face, and looked deeply into my eyes as I looked into his. He then touched the left side of his forehead to mine, and we quietly remained in this position for what others later described as two or three minutes. For me, it was timeless because I'd suspended any inquiry or thought about what was happening and simply went with the experience. Those moments changed my life forever.

With my eyes closed and His Holiness's head joined with mine, I became acutely aware of my heart. The image that was projected into my consciousness was an aerial view of two large doors beginning to slowly swing outward until they were completely open.

28

Feelings of peace, happiness, and deep love for all humanity and the world around us quietly flowed into my awareness. At that moment, I knew that no matter what happened to me personally or to the universe at large, my heart would always remain open, for that was who I truly was. There was no longer any fear or doubt that I would find my way Home.

At the end of this time, the Dalai Lama once again looked deeply into my eyes, and we both smiled with knowing joy about what had occurred.

I'm sure that many others have had even more profound experiences than I did and as devout Buddhists are much more deserving of them. However, one of the many lessons I learned that day is that people don't have to be theologically aligned to share a spiritual understanding. In fact, religious dogma can sometimes interfere with the possibilities for joining.

All I know for sure is that on that day, overlooking the Pacific Ocean in Santa Barbara, a monk from a distant land and a foreign religion facilitated one of the most important spiritual experiences of my life . . . and for him and that encounter, I'll always be grateful.

Often the most important signposts for finding our way Home to our Source are the least expected. What's labeled "foreign," "different," or "not like me" is often that which we have yet to meet, know, or cherish. Having an open heart allows Love to enter through many doors.

My Rearview Mirror

— Jerry

I was driving my 12-year-old yellow Honda Civic when I went over a large bump in the road. To my surprise, the rearview mirror fell to the floor of the car and broke. Since nothing like this had ever happened to me before, I immediately pulled to the side of the road to ponder whether there might be some lesson in this unexpected event.

I became quiet and stilled my mind. Then I started to chuckle because a little voice inside me asked, *Jerry, when are you going to stop looking backward in your life?* After I stopped laughing, my first thought was that God has a wonderful sense of humor.

At the time, I *had* felt stuck on several issues from long ago—and whenever I dwell on something from the past, I find that I'm unhappy, conflicted, and ultimately depressed. As I drove home, each time I glanced at the empty spot where my rearview mirror used to hang, I was glad to see it missing, because it reminded me that *I* was not my past.

*Unhappy memories can only hurt us if we choose
to relive them in the present. The greatest happiness
comes to those who choose peace in this moment.*

Why Am I Here?

— Diane

The first university workshop Jerry and I gave together was in 1984 at the University of California's Irvine campus. We arrived about half an hour early and were given a brochure about the weekend program. It was then that I felt the stirring of a conflict within: My name wasn't there—only Jerry was listed as a presenter. All my fears and nervousness about not feeling that I belonged there came to a head.

"That does it. I didn't want to come here in the first place. No one wants to hear me speak—this just confirms that I'm not supposed to be on the program. I'm not going in. You do this yourself," I told Jerry.

"Okay," he answered, "but you know, Diane, even if your name *was* on the program, you could still choose not to go in."

"That's fine," I replied with a nervous quiver in my voice, "because I'm *not*."

"You need to know that I'm not attached to your giving the workshop with me, and I'm sorry they omitted your name—but may I ask you one question?" I replied that he could. "Why did you come here today?"

I hesitated, thought for a moment, and then responded in a softer, less fearful voice, "I came here to give love."

"Do you think you're capable of doing that?" he inquired.

"Yes, I *know* I can do *that*."

Then Jerry looked deep into my eyes and in his gentle way said the words that changed my life: "Diane, that's all you'll *ever* be required to do." He began to get up, adding, "I'm going inside now, and you may decide to join me on the stage or in the audience, or I'll see you at the end of the day. Either way, please know that I love you."

Jerry went in while I pondered his question and my answer. Knowing that I was capable of giving love, I decided to enter the hall and join him onstage. It was a truly transformative experience for both of us. People spoke of their fears, and I talked of mine and my experience that morning. Throughout the day, we were *all* teachers and students for each other. The subject of the workshop was: "Love Is the Answer No Matter What the Question!"

Reminding ourselves daily why we're here focuses our
minds on the true purpose of our existence: to love each other,
to grow, and to give and receive comfort. We can't control other
people, situations, or outcomes—much as we try to—but we can
keep our minds focused on love. If we do that much, our
path will be more peaceful and our way more certain.

The Green Car

—Diane

Jerry and I were consulting for San Francisco General Hospital's AIDS program. Parking is usually difficult there, so I generally arrive half an hour early to find a place. On one particular day, I was delighted to find a spot near the front entrance, something that had never happened before.

The two-hour Attitudinal Healing session went quite well. We emphasized that we can always choose peace instead of conflict, and that it's only our thoughts and attitudes that hurt us. Following the session, I went to my vehicle, only to find that a large green car had parked sideways behind me and was blocking my way. I thought, *Oh well, this person has just run in for a brief errand and is sure to return in a minute or two.*

The "minute or two" stretched into 20, and then 40. I was getting panicked. Maybe the owner of the green car was there for an eight-hour shift! I became very upset because in 30 minutes I was supposed to be across town for a presentation and had no way to contact the attendees. If the driver of the green car didn't come soon, I wouldn't make it.

I noticed that with each person who came close to the green car, I got angrier and angrier, until I was in a frazzled state. I then reminded myself of what we'd just been discussing at the meeting about being able to choose peace on the inside regardless of what's happening in the external world. And you know what? It made absolutely no difference whatsoever! I was convinced that I was right—the innocent victim of an inconsiderate person. I was also confident that most people would line up behind me to support this belief.

As the minutes ticked by, I went from anger to outrage. I caught myself and thought, *Diane, you're acting deranged!* I decided to sit there for a few more minutes and get very quiet mentally. Then I said to myself, *I absolutely don't know what's going on here, but there must be something I can learn from this.*

What came into my mind was the lesson Jerry and I had just spent two hours discussing: *I can choose peace over conflict.* Was I a victim, or could I still choose to experience tranquility? I then said aloud, "Okay, I choose peace." I became very quiet and stilled my mind. What emerged from deep inside me was that I should ask the next person I saw if he or she knew anything about the green car.

A few moments went by, and when a man came out of the building, I called out to him, "Excuse me, but could you tell me anything about this green car?"

"Oh, yes," he replied. "Just go around to the front of the building to the right, through the front door, down the hall, and into the last office on the right. They'll be able to tell you about the green car."

I was amazed. I went into the building, but as I was a little confused about his directions, I asked in the first office I saw if anyone knew anything about the green car. Without looking up, two workers simultaneously replied, "Yes." One of them said: "Just go down the hall and into the last door on the right, and they can tell you about the green car."

By this time I was fascinated and had totally calmed down. I actually felt very peaceful inside. I knew that I really had no idea what was going on in the outside world just then. I walked into the office as directed, where there was a woman sitting at a desk and a man standing beside it. I said very calmly, "Excuse me, but can you tell me about the green car double-parked outside?"

The man replied pleasantly, "That's my car."

Gently, I said, "Well, you know the gray car you're blocking next to the building? That's mine, and I was wondering if you could take a few minutes to move your car so I can get out."

The woman behind the desk said, "Excuse me, but did you know that you parked in a police tow-away zone?"

Completely shocked, I finally spoke, answering in a timid voice, "Well, no, I didn't know that."

The man then asked, "And did you know that we *are* the police?"

"No, I didn't know that either!"

He looked at me and smiled. "You know," he said, "we were just saying that when the person who owns the gray car storms in here, ranting and raving, we're going to have it towed anyway. But you came in and were so nice that I'll be glad to move my car."

As we walked toward the parking lot together, the man explained, "Several times a day we tow cars that have parked there, or at the very least, we ticket them. But I must tell you that this time something inside me said to just wait for the person with the gray car. That's why I blocked it in order to see who it was—and I'm glad I did."

"You wouldn't believe what went through my mind," I responded. And then I told him the whole story. Before I got into my car to leave, we hugged each other.

As I drove away, I found myself thinking about what a wonderful lesson this had been. I'd been so certain that I was right and felt so justified in my indignation. I also remembered all the other times in my life when I was so sure that I was right and someone else was wrong.

It's easy to let our egos take charge of our minds and to blame others for the problems we encounter. However, any situation can reflect love if we choose peace rather than conflict . . . even though it may require a sustained effort to do so.

35

Calligraphy as a Teacher of Stillness

— Jerry

In 1976, I realized that I was rushing through life. My pattern was to make a huge to-do list each morning, then charge through the day attempting to accomplish everything I'd set out to do. I knew that I needed to put the brakes on this "normal" pace, so I decided to try something that seemed unattainable but might help me slow down. I started taking calligraphy lessons.

I realized that this would also improve another area of my life: my handwriting, which had always been a scribble that no one could read. Perhaps that's one of the reasons I got in to medical school, since most people can't read their physician's writing! The calligraphy forced me to breathe slowly, remain in the present, and practice stillness—all of which also helped me to remember God.

To demonstrate that nothing is impossible, I wrote a Christmas letter as a gift to each of my two sons, sharing my appreciation and love for them . . . and I wrote both in calligraphy. This blew their socks off because they could actually read what I'd written!

After Christmas my handwriting slipped back into being a scribble again, and I found myself returning to my old "hurried energy" mode. I needed something that would allow me to develop better discipline, so I went to the bank and told them that I wanted to change my signature to one written in calligraphy. The bank manager was concerned that somebody could easily copy it. When I told him that my calligraphy signature helped remind me of God, I think he decided that I was a bit crazy, but he went along with my decision.

A few months later, I was visiting my parents in Los Angeles. They'd recently moved and wanted my signature on their safe-deposit box. As I was signing my name in calligraphy, my mother shouted at me, "That's not your signature! Why are you writing like that?!" I tried to explain that it slowed me up and helped me remember God. She cut in, "If you want to remember God, do it in your own house. When you're in mine, scribble your signature like you always have!"

This wasn't the first or the last time I noticed that my mother felt threatened by any change in my behavior. As always, she served as a powerful reminder that people don't have to fit into a certain form for me to love them. She taught me a lot about acceptance, forgiveness, and letting go of expectations.

Rushing through life at breakneck speed, meeting one deadline after another, makes it impossible to experience inner peace. It's a choice to slow down, still our minds, and relax into the present, even if it's only for a moment at a time.

Walls Do Not
a Prison Make

— Diane

In the mid-'80s, Jerry and I were invited by the Sai Organization to lecture in Phoenix, Arizona. The foundation was honoring individuals who weren't part of the organization but had demonstrated exemplary community service, and we'd been asked to talk about Attitudinal Healing. Robert Muller, the former assistant secretary general at the United Nations and a dear friend, was selected to lecture in the eastern United States, while we were picked for the West.

During the talk, we told the story of an Arizona inmate who wrote Jerry to tell him that *Love Is Letting Go of Fear* was the worst book he'd ever read. He said that in the penitentiary near Phoenix where he was incarcerated, he'd been beaten by guards and put in solitary confinement, and consequently didn't believe in forgiveness. He ended the letter by saying that Jerry was a "flaky" psychiatrist from California who didn't know anything about real life.

Jerry answered with a nondefensive letter, and the two men became pen pals. Six months later when Jerry was scheduled to speak in Phoenix, he visited the man at the prison. He told Jerry that he was considered the worst inmate there, and that although he'd originally been sentenced to three years, because of his behavior the term had been lengthened to seven.

He said that his mother was a prostitute, and his father was an alcoholic. He complained about several other individuals in his life as well. Jerry told him that if he continued to blame others for what had happened, he might never get out; but if he chose to change his belief system, it was possible for him to be released sooner.

A short time after returning home, Jerry received a letter from the man saying that he'd finally realized what the books and letters were really about. He added that he'd discovered that what was keeping him in this angry bondage wasn't the walls of the prison, the guards, his parents, or his past; it was the fear and blame he kept re-creating in the present in his own mind.

Further letters showed that he was beginning to take responsibility for his behavior, and within three and a half years, he was released from prison. Jerry told the audience that in the intervening years he'd lost contact with the man.

Immediately after we finished telling this story, people stood up and clapped. Unbeknownst to us, since his release, Jerry's former pen pal had become quite well known in the newspapers for his good work with both inmates and those who had been released from prison. The reason why people were giving a standing ovation wasn't because of us, but because the man also happened to be in the audience, and many of them had already recognized him there! In talking with him after the lecture, we learned that he was also volunteering much of his time helping those who had been diagnosed with cancer and other life-threatening illnesses and were facing the possibility of death.

Blaming others keeps us in a mental prison from which there's no escape. Miracles occur when we turn from anger and judgment to embrace forgiveness.

$\mathscr{G}$uilty in Japan

— Jerry

During a lecture tour in Japan, we were giving a workshop at the Tokyo International Trade Center. I had the idea of asking the participants to write what they felt most guilty about on a piece of paper. Those who were willing to see that guilt was hindering them and wanted to let go of it were to bring the paper to me.

I asked the first volunteer to put her paper in a large ashtray. I then lit a match to it so that we could watch the guilt disappear along with the paper. Unfortunately, though, that's not exactly what happened!

The hotel's fire-alarm system was extremely sensitive and went off with a noise loud enough to blast us out of the room. Security personnel appeared from every direction as we all sat frozen, with eyes fixed upward to see if the sprinkler system would be set off. It wasn't, but in spite of trying to help others get rid of their negative emotions, the day began with *me* feeling guilty. Minds are very complex indeed. And I say this as the author of a book solely on the subject of guilt: *We are all works in progress!*

After the drama of the fire was "extinguished," people began sharing why they'd come to a workshop on Attitudinal Healing. Diane and I had been told that the Japanese are very reserved and would find it difficult to share personal feelings. That assessment quickly went out the window when an elegantly dressed woman introduced herself as a high-priced prostitute who had come that day to find a way of changing her life.

There was a brief silence, then the older woman sitting next to her said, "You know, I've never thought about this before, but I believe I'm also a prostitute, because the only reason I stay married to my husband is because of his money. I too want to change how I live."

Our intention in every workshop is to create an environment where people don't have to worry about being judged and where we can learn from one another's pain, fears, failures, and successes. The experience then becomes a guide for the atmosphere we can all create for each other in our daily lives.

Never underestimate the ego's attraction to guilt.
Perhaps it even seems virtuous to dwell on our mistakes, but
it's impossible to experience inner peace and shame at the same
time. Saying good-bye to guilt and replacing it with love opens
our hearts to healing . . . for others and for ourselves.

A Message from the Sky

— Diane

Jerry and I love to greet the day by taking a walk on the beach in Kailua, Oahu, just before the sun comes up. We have an agreement that we'll only relate internally to nature and contemplate spiritual matters for the first half of our walk, so we don't speak during that time. Once we head home, it's okay to talk.

One day as we began the second half of our walk, I shared some angry feelings I was holding on to regarding something that had happened to me three different times recently. Jerry asked if I really believed that our thoughts create our reality. While I knew intellectually that his question was valid, my emotions were running high as I responded in a rather loud voice, "Not this time—this is the exception!" Then I said a word I rarely use, "I feel as though I've been *sh*-- upon!"

Within a nanosecond, literally before I'd taken three steps, a big glob of bird sh-- fell from the sky and hit me, landing on my left breast in a neat pile right over my heart. In decades of walking beaches, this had never happened to me before. I was so stunned that I stopped in my tracks. I looked at Jerry and he looked at me, and we both looked at the sh--.

Jerry couldn't resist quietly commenting, "I hope you noticed, Diane, that the bird didn't sh-- on me."

We both burst out laughing as I threw my hands in the air and shouted: "Okay, okay! I get it, I get it! My thoughts *do* create my reality!"

*Our thoughts create our reality. What we believe is
what we see. There are no idle thoughts—simply because
they aren't visible doesn't make them unimportant. A peaceful,
loving mind creates a more harmonious reality. Remember
that we may not be able to change a situation or another
person, but we can <u>always</u> change our thoughts.*

Where There Is Love, There Is a Way

— Jerry and Diane

In 1982, we began a ten-year journey through nearly 30 countries to provide AIDS education. We worked cross-culturally among grassroots organizations and medical communities to highlight the psychological, social, and spiritual aspects of how the disease was affecting all strata of society.

During the '80s, we were also working within the Soviet Union on our decadelong project Children as Teachers of Peace, in which we brought kids from one country to another to help bridge the gap between perceived enemies. During our trips to the USSR, we also inquired about the effect of AIDS in that part of the world. The government continually denied any presence of the disease, but we discovered a clinic on the outskirts of Moscow that held incarcerated people infected with the deadly virus. With the immeasurable assistance of Russian-language expert Carolyn Smith, we gained the trust of the doctors and gradually trained a few of them in the Principles of Attitudinal Healing and in the powerful potential of support groups based on people healing together. This was the seed for the founding of the Moscow Center for Attitudinal Healing.

While at the AIDS clinic, a mother very cautiously approached us and informed us that Alexie, her five-year-old son, needed an operation to correct his malformed gastrointestinal organs, defective from birth. The problem, she explained, was that no doctors would operate on her son because he'd contracted the AIDS virus through a tainted blood transfusion shortly after being born. She pleaded with us to take him to the U.S. for this complicated operation.

Since these were the earliest days of glasnost, which was the start of the thaw in Soviet-American relations, Soviet citizens were rarely allowed to leave the country. Additionally, the strict U.S. immigration laws pertaining to Russians made fulfilling her plea seem impossible. However, when we asked for guidance, we clearly got a *yes* to proceed. In doing so, we had to let go of *how* we would accomplish this and simply have confidence that a way would become clear.

Getting Alexie and his mother out of their country proved much easier than getting them into ours. With help from the mayor of San Francisco, friends at San Francisco General Hospital's AIDS Ward 5A, and the Jewish Community Center, we were able to bring them to California, where Alexie underwent surgery. Housing was a challenge, since they didn't speak any English. Carolyn, also a facilitator of the children's group at our Center in nearby Sausalito, continued to assist us in this effort, as well as in all of our subsequent Soviet experiences.

While trying to help Alexie and his mother find their way back to Moscow, we were shocked when the doctors, all of whom had donated their skills and time, announced that they would have to perform a second operation. They needed about nine months between the surgeries for him to heal internally. What to do was the question.

If we sent them back, we couldn't be assured that they would be able to leave their country or reenter ours a second time. We finally decided to offer to keep them in San Francisco for the entire time. This proved difficult for everyone, including Alexie's mother, who had left her other children at home. Through the generosity of many, especially Catholic Charities, who housed and fed them, what previously seemed impossible became possible.

The second operation was successful, and Alexie and his mother returned to Moscow with a little English and a lot of love.

The lesson for us was: "When you reach into the darkness to help another back into the light, you discover that the hand you grasp is your own." Assisting them helped all of us open our hearts even more.

*When we listen to our inner guidance and make
a commitment based on it, what might seem impossible
can become reality. When we commit to being truly helpful,
others will join us. And when we extend love to others,
we're shown the direction for our own journey.*

A Travel Guide

— Diane

Jerry and I always pray about whether to accept a speaking invitation, and that's how our travel plans are choreographed. Once, we received two invitations for the same day: The first was for a one-day event in New York City that didn't include much information as to the purpose; the other was a seven-week trip to Australia.

Having grown up in New York and never having been to Australia, I knew which invitation *I* really wanted to accept. Jerry had previously lectured Down Under and had expressed a desire to go back. What could be clearer or more perfect? With great excitement, I exclaimed, "Let's go to Australia!"

Jerry calmly replied, "Diane, we agreed that we would always pray about what we should do. Don't you think we ought to pray on this, too?" I reluctantly agreed.

We closed our eyes and prayed. I tried to imagine the letters *A-U-S-T-R-A-L-I-A* spelled out across my inner mind, but to my shock, I got *New York*. Incredibly disappointed, I asked Jerry what he'd received. When he replied, "New York," I quickly suggested, "Let's pray again!" Once more, we got *New York,* and on that basis we turned down the invitation to Australia.

It took three weeks for us to obtain more information about the event, which turned out to be a huge gathering at the Cathedral

Church of St. John the Divine, sponsored by a nongovernmental arm of the United Nations. Religious and spiritual leaders from all over the world would be attending. Because of our work with Children as Teachers of Peace, the committee organizers asked us to bring 40 kids from different countries. We wound up inviting children of personnel who worked at the United Nations.

The event was quite extraordinary. After we made a few introductory remarks, three of the children talked about what peace meant to them. At the end of the evening, all of our kids went around the church lighting the candles that had been given to the 12,000 people in attendance. It was one of the most sacred and profound moments for us and, I imagine, everyone there.

My ego mind had wanted to go to Australia, but as Jerry and I stood there together watching the candlelight spread through that beautiful cathedral sanctuary, I knew that we were exactly where we were supposed to be. The following year we were once again invited to Australia, and we were guided to go there (and to New Zealand) on a life-changing adventure.

*Making healthy decisions is helped by stilling
our minds, opening our hearts, and coming
with empty hands to listen for the answer.*

Letting Go of Categorization

— Jerry

Several years ago I was in New York to give a lecture. I'd been invited to a rather large cocktail party but didn't particularly want to go, having assumed that I'd just get caught up in small talk. After struggling over what to do, I decided that the most loving thing would be to attend.

I arrived about 45 minutes late, saw an empty couch, and headed straight for it. Just as I'd seated myself, another man sat down next to me. We began talking and quickly became involved in a conversation that covered a wide range of interesting topics. We found ourselves enjoying each other's company immensely.

Eventually our hostess came over and told us how happy she was that we'd gotten together. She then asked, "By the way, you've introduced yourselves and told each other what you do, haven't you?"

"No," we both responded.

She then introduced me as a psychiatrist from California, whereupon the man sitting next to me jumped up with fire in his eyes and exclaimed, "I *hate* psychiatrists!"

Ignoring his outburst, our hostess introduced my companion as a famous pianist. I immediately stated that although I enjoyed music, in no way did I consider myself an expert on it, and if I'd known who he was, I probably would have gotten up and walked away out of fear of saying something stupid.

At this point, we all laughed, and the pianist and I continued to talk. Both of us remarked how upon first meeting an individual and asking, "What do you do?" the response we receive often determines whether we want to continue the conversation.

When we categorize people, we're tempted to
make judgments about them. Doing so always
prevents us from enjoying an individual, a relationship,
or a conversation, because we only see our own judgment.
Even if our assessment is that the other person is in some
way superior to us, judgment is still separating. To be
free of it in all forms is to be open to a feeling of
equality and to experiencing the present moment.

Valentine's Day

— Jerry

In late January several years ago, I decided to visit the Attitudinal Healing Support Group at The Redwoods retirement home in Mill Valley, California.

After meditating, I got the idea of bringing roses to all of the 12 participants, whose ages ranged from 66 to 93. As I gave each person a flower, I hugged him or her. I was surprised by how deeply this little gift affected the members of the group. Some of them said that they hadn't received any flowers for years. Others couldn't remember *ever* having gotten any.

It occurred to me that if a rose and a hug could have this kind of effect, why not do the same for all 250 residents on Valentine's Day? I convinced a nursery to donate the roses and a bottling company to donate bottles to put them in, all of which were to arrive at The Redwoods on February 14. I then enlisted a dozen children between the ages of 7 and 12 to come to the retirement home after school to give each of the residents a hug along with a rose.

We arrived at the scheduled time, only to find that the bottles were full of carbonated water! Since we didn't have time to empty them, we took off the caps and stuck a rose into each one.

It's impossible to express the power of love I witnessed that day between those children and the senior citizens. The kids didn't rush away, but rather stayed and chatted for a while, as if a generational divide had somehow been bridged. As we were leaving, they even asked me when they could come back and visit again!

A few days later, several residents—with huge smiles on their faces—told us that roses obviously last much longer when they're kept in carbonated water!

When given with love, the smallest gift has transformative power. And when accompanied by a hug, it can be magical.

$\mathcal{M}$y Workaholism

— Diane

Over the years, I've gotten caught up in several unhelpful mind-sets, but none has been as protracted as workaholism, which possessed me everywhere I went. There were entire years when I worked 14 hours each day, every day. This pace slowly depleted my reserves of mental and physical energy. To say that my life suffered from a lack of balance seems laughably obvious. Outside of work, I simply didn't *have* a life. But why did I get into such a state?

One of the reasons why I adopted this mind-set is because my mother and father grew up during the Great Depression, and their parents had to work two or three jobs just to make ends meet. When I was growing up, my own parents had to do nearly the same. A pervasive belief in my family was that working hard made you a good person. As a child, I assumed that if you didn't give everything your all, you were "not good enough" as a human being.

Children tend to emulate their parents and adopt their values, especially if they equate them with being loved. Consequently, when I ventured into work of any kind, I gave 100 percent . . . *plus* whatever else was necessary to assure success. Even though the results didn't always manifest themselves in the way I planned, I nevertheless searched for personal validity in the final outcome.

Not surprisingly, the business partners I picked also had the same proclivity for long hours and hard work. They supported my unbalanced life and behavior with their own.

The public workplace and an unbalanced life can easily hide private feelings, and I ran so fast and kept so busy that I was able to escape the internal unresolved chaos of my childhood—or so I thought. In reality, the unhealed places of my heart leaked out over every aspect of my life. I kept my relationships more superficial in order to safeguard myself from the depth of my sadness. My work, while successful on the outside, felt like failure to me on the inside. And my spiritual life was split, just as I was, between my inner reality and the surrounding cocoon of endless work.

To this day, I struggle with the need to shift my life away from self-imposed workloads and toward open space and free time. Whenever I fail to consciously stop my merry-go-round, I feel increasingly frantic and I separate from my true self and those around me. Far more often than before, I'm now making choices that transform my immersion in workaholism into a holistic outlook that nurtures not only my mind, but my body and spirit as well.

A hurried and busy mind has no room
for spiritual experiences. There's limitless
value in stillness and an unhurried pace.

An ancient saying from India states: "A busy
mind is a sick mind, a slow mind is a healthy
mind, and a still mind is a Divine mind."

Intuitive Ways of Knowing

— Diane

Most of us have experienced knowing something at "the gut level" and acting on it successfully. Many interpretations have been given in an attempt to explain this phenomenon, but perhaps the most common comment is: "I have absolutely no idea *how* it works—I just know that it *does.*"

Years ago, I decided to test the premise that we have access to information beyond our five senses. It was my first time driving in the downtown area of a major city, and I only had an address and no directions. This was pre-MapQuest days, and I was unfamiliar with the street signs and identifying landmarks. Unable to reach the people at my destination by phone, I found myself in a quandary, since I had a set appointment time but had no idea how to get there.

There was a moment after I entered the city when I felt an inner sense of panic. My ego definitely doesn't like being geographically lost, and I pride myself on being good at finding my way. I remember pulling off the highway, not even knowing where to exit. I then had an experience that created a paradigm shift in the way I make decisions.

Sitting in my car, I had the thought that in my heart of hearts, I believed we all have access to intuitive ways of knowing things that defy common methods of gathering information. So why not apply that belief now? If I was right, I should be able to tap into all the driving directions I needed. Somewhat excited, I decided to try.

After returning to the highway, I asked the question: *What do I need to know?* Shortly thereafter, I had a strong sense that I should exit on a particular street. At the stoplight, I had no idea which way to turn, so I asked, *Right or left?* And somehow I just *knew* that I should go right. I then proceeded to the next corner and did the same thing, this time being guided to turn left. As I entered the belly of the city, I became fascinated to see if indeed this course of inquiry would lead me to my destination. This went on for about 15 minutes as I was directed eastward.

Suddenly I got nothing. I repeated my question over and over, but only silence greeted me. I remember losing my enthusiasm and actually chiding myself about what a farce this exercise was. I opened my window and asked a passerby if he had any idea where the address was. A bit confused, he looked at me and said, "Well, it's right here." Pointing behind him, he explained, "This is the entrance to the garage for the building around the corner that you're looking for."

*We all have intuitive ways of knowing things about
our lives and the those of others. Accessing this knowledge
is a matter of conscious choice and practice, combined with
the belief that it's possible. Such knowledge provides us with
another way of making decisions that is based on nontraditional
means of accessing information and spiritual guidance.*

$\mathcal{K}eil\ Cove$

— *Jerry*

The rent for my apartment had been drastically increased and I needed to move. I imagined the kind of place I wanted: secluded, filled with trees, and close to nature—a home that would provide a peaceful environment in which to live and write. Diane was living in Belvedere.

One Sunday afternoon when Diane and I were congratulating each other because we'd just finished editing our book *Love Is the Answer,* I suddenly received inner guidance that I shared with her. We were to take a walk, where we would encounter someone who would be of help in finding a new place to live. Ten minutes later, we crossed paths with a woman I hadn't seen in years, who told us that she and her husband had just purchased a house down the street from where I was currently living. After showing us her new home and finding out about my search for one, she said she knew the perfect place: It was located in Keil Cove, not far from where we were standing.

The 40-acre property was magical, with its own beach on San Francisco Bay. There were more than a hundred species of birds, old redwood trees, hiking trails, and even a small lake in front of the 100-year-old cottage that was for rent. We met the owners, who told us that they were sorry, but they'd just leased it the day before.

As we began to walk away, Diane turned to look at the cottage across the lake and stopped me to say that she saw us living there—literally, she saw an image of us in front of the cottage. Her remark surprised me because up until that point we'd lived in separate houses. While I was thoroughly delighted by the "us" part, I nonetheless put on my "psychiatric hat" and told her that we needed to accept reality and move on because the cottage wasn't available. Diane was quite insistent that she truly saw us living there, and her guidance was that we not look for another place for at least a week. I agreed to this.

Four days later, we received a call from the cottage's owner to tell us that the prospective tenant's contract couldn't proceed because the escrow for the house he was selling had fallen through. (We later discovered that the house was right next to where I lived.) The owner said that the cottage was ours if we still wanted it. Diane and I assured him that we did.

Diane's theory was that the Housing Fairy had come to visit us on a foggy night, had mistakenly waved her magic wand over the wrong house, and then had come back to correct the error. We were married shortly thereafter and, thanks to the graciousness of two generations of the Keil Family, lived our next 14 years in that very special place.

Inner guidance is available to all of us. It can't be used to meet our ego desires, and it doesn't provide us with a charmed life . . . but it does give us something much more important: a sense of Divine connection. It's a gift from One Who loves us and wishes us well. The willingness to consult our inner guide is among the most important choices we can make on our spiritual journey. To be open to the voice of "I" is to be open to experiencing the seemingly impossible as possible after all.

The Seashore

— Jerry

The seashore has always felt like a second home to me. For most of my childhood in Long Beach, California, I lived just two blocks from the beach, where I bodysurfed and swam.

For more than 40 years, my office in Tiburon was at the end of a dock over the water on San Francisco Bay. My home for 14 years was on pilings looking out at Angel Island. For a decade and a half, Diane and I lived at Keil Cove, which was located on a small lake just 20 yards from the bay. We now spend half our time on a houseboat on San Francisco Bay and the other half on the beach in Hawaii.

The sea has always been like a magnet pulling me to it. The ripples of the waves soothe my heart, and the ocean breeze nourishes my soul. At the beach, the water kissing the sand brings home the mystery, beauty, and sacredness of nature.

When Diane and I walk by the shore, we get away from the business of the world and dwell on those things that remind us of the interconnection of the universe. It's as if all of our senses are in harmony with the light and beauty around us. We're one with each other, and we feel the presence of Spirit. Our footprints in the sand remind us that the only steps of progress are those of forgiveness.

When we walk away from the sun, we notice our shadows; and when we walk toward it, we see none . . . which reminds us to choose the Light wherever we go.

The world is distracting, and our egos are stubborn.
It requires focus and determination to concentrate
on love. Having a place that nurtures the soul and
feeds the spirit symbolizes our Home and helps
remind us of where and what we truly are.

Grandkids

— Jerry and Diane

We were thinking about how much we love and appreciate our four grandchildren—Jacquelyn, Grant, Jalena, and Lexi Jampolsky. They each continue to bless and nourish our lives in their own unique way.

Wanting to express our feelings and what we wished them to remember, we wrote the following poem and sent it to them with all our love. Because it came from our affectionate caring, we wanted to share it with *all* the grandchildren and children in the world and with the wonderful, innocent child that resides in each of our adult hearts, waiting to be remembered.

These are the thoughts we would
choose to have you remember,
now and forevermore.

Remember every day, every moment,
and every second of your life that
you are Love.
This is your true identity
and everything that you are.

You are all that is beautiful and more.
You are every rose, every tulip, every lily, every
orchid, every gardenia—every flower.
You are the fragrance of all the flowers in the
world united as one.

And please, please, remember this:
Never doubt for even one instant,
no matter what anybody might say,
that you are all that
is beautiful . . . and more.

Being Love, you are precious.
You are all that is beyond magnificent.
You are what is beyond all form.
You are the reflection of the full moon
and the stars at night.

You are the Light of the sun
that warms all hearts, whoever
or wherever they may be.

Make all your decisions in life
based on Love rather than fear.
Follow your heart
and Love will always follow you
wherever you go.

Trust in Love and forgiveness.
Have faith in possibilities
and trust the invisible
and you will never be
far from Home.

In the school of life,
Love is more important
than reading, writing, or arithmetic.

Love is the answer to
any problem
you will ever face.

Children are the
best, the freest, huggers
in the world.
And we all
need more hugging.
You cannot love too much.
You cannot hug too much.

Become a Teacher of Love
and Hugging for
the rest of your life
and your heart will sing
with happiness every step
that you take.

We came into the world full of love, joy, radiance, and innocence, only to assume the heavy mantles of our separate ways. Children are shining lights who remind us of what we so frequently forget: that there is an innocence in each of us.

Finding My Roots

— Diane

While lecturing in Europe a number of years ago, we found ourselves with two open days—something that's a rarity for us on speaking tours. When we were discussing what to do with this little gift, Jerry suggested that we fly to the island of Sicily at the southernmost tip of Italy. Knowing that I had very little knowledge of my paternal grandparents' families and that I also wanted news and information to bring back to my aging aunts and uncle, he proposed that we fly to the capital, Palermo, to attempt to discover my roots.

Although I'd taken four years of Latin in high school and three years of Spanish, I'd forgotten most of this knowledge. My attempt to communicate in Italian at the airport was pathetic. No one was able to understand a thing I tried to get across, with the exception of a few hand gestures. A short while later, an angel named Rosalba appeared and in slightly accented English said, "I will help you find your family. It would be my pleasure." Despite numerous attempts to pay her, she refused any money. The next two days unfolded like a tapestry as the three of us tried to weave 91 years of family fragments into a whole fabric.

The name Cirincione may seem rare to most who first hear it, but there are hundreds of people by that name in Sicily, as we discovered when we looked in the island's phone book. What *was* helpful was that only 19 spelled it with one *r* instead of two.

We visited a picturesque mountain village, where I saw some-one from the car who looked *exactly* like my father as a young man, a Robert De Niro look. I began to get really excited about the possibilities. We convinced the parish priest to let us see the church records of births, marriages, and deaths. After hours of investigative work, we discovered that there were three lines of Cirinciones, but none of them in this village were related to me. Since Italian family names are passed on generation after genera-tion, it was easy to track the lines of descent. Unlike the others in the village, mine came from Joseph, John, and Andrew.

After calling 18 Cirinciones in the phone book, we had no leads as to families who might have had members come to New York City via Ellis Island in the early 1900s. Our last hope, num-ber 19—a doctor from the beautiful coastal town of Cefalù—also seemed like a dead end. But just as we were about to hang up with him and end the quest, he said, "Once, while dining in Palermo, I met a woman named Ellen who owned the restaurant. She said that some of her family immigrated around 1902," but he added that he thought they spelled their name with two *r*'s instead of one. This being the only lead we had left, we followed it to the woman's place of work.

Ellen was excited to meet me because a few years before, a cousin in Canada and another in France had sent her our book *Love Is the Answer*. They assumed that we were related but didn't know how to contact me. She also stated that some of her family members had indeed emigrated, and that while she now spelled her name with two *r*'s, she was born with only one and was mis-takenly given the second *r* when she made her first Holy Com-munion at age seven. Since most people spelled their names that way and there were very few with a single *r*, she never bothered to change it back.

Feeling quite hopeful, we joined her on a visit to several of her older relatives to see if there was any connection, but we hit another dead end. They told us that most of the families who immigrated to Ellis Island in New York at that time came from Bagheria, a suburb of Palermo. With just hours left in our two-day window, off we went to investigate this lovely town by the sea.

Not knowing where to begin, Jerry had another brilliant idea. He said, "Let's find the oldest living Cirincione and see what he or she remembers." We did so, and found ourselves in the formal parlor of a 94-year-old woman. We tried to piece together our family histories but were unable to find an actual connection. I felt as if this was finally the end of our trail, and my heart sank.

As we sat in this woman's parlor, sipping tea and preparing to leave for the airport, I happened to glance upward toward the unusually high ceiling. Each wall had two portraits (eight altogether) of her relatives from generations past. I studied their faces, pointed to one, and asked, "Who is that?"

The woman said that he was Dr. Joseph Cirincione, the father of Italian ophthalmology. I began to get excited because this was the first name in my family tree that we'd actually found, and it was my uncle's and great-grandfather's name as well. I then pointed to the portrait of a woman and inquired about her identity.

"She is Josephina Solerno. Many of the Cirinciones married the Solernos, and a few of them moved to America during very hard times here."

I said, "My paternal grandmother's name was Solerno; and her daughter, my aunt, was named Josephine. This is my family."

With only moments left, we visited Villa Cirincione and the local family who had inherited it. The daughter was Kathryn Cirincione—my grandmother's, cousins', and sister's name. They told us that when Dr. Joseph Cirincione visited from Rome, where he taught at the university, he used to give free eye care to the local families. He was widely known for having resisted the dictator Mussolini and for helping the poor.

The patriarch of the family told us that his grandfather and his brothers worked in the churches in Palermo, restoring the paintings and stained-glass windows. I knew little of my family, but I'd heard that this was also my great-grandfather's profession. He also spoke of a family-lineage chart that he remembered seeing at age 12, just before it was stolen, which traced the ancestry in detail back to northern Italy in 1594. He clearly recalled that the first name on the chart was Andrea (Andrew), my brother's and grandfather's name. All the names in the family were ours. This was a joyous reunion.

Visiting Sicily allowed me to return home and share some of the missing pieces of our heritage with my father's family, bridging the 91-year disconnect that had left us all wondering where we came from. Jerry's suggestion had been priceless because of the abundant fruit of connection that it bore. At the time, I thought that I was seeking my physical source, my history—but now, because of the seeming gaps in wholeness that it filled, I see it as part of the journey to find my way Home to my spiritual Source.

Our worldly identities can appear to have many faces, but in the end it's the search for our true Self that leads us Home.

$\mathscr{A}$ Blank Piece of Paper

— *Diane*

Throughout most of my life, I didn't consider myself artistically talented. Although I developed some abilities—in fashion design, for example—I felt limited in the expression of fine arts such as drawing, painting, and sculpting, despite the fact that I never delved seriously into any of them.

I've come to realize that the younger child in a family often feels "less than" in areas where an older sibling excels, even when there's no overt reason for the feeling. The ego deduces that "[s]he is so artistic smart/athletic/good at _____ [fill in the blank], I therefore must not be." This rarely has anything to do with the older sibling; rather, it's usually an unconscious inner process on the part of the younger one. Some younger children become very competitive and often excel above the older one, while others accept a view of themselves as inevitably inferior. When it came to art, I embraced the latter perception.

One of the ways I expressed my lack of artistic confidence was to overwork everything I created because I didn't feel that it was ever good enough to be complete. The critical voice in my head kept saying, *If you just do this or that, it will be better.* I did this to the point of overkill, and rather than showing my creation to anyone, I invariably destroyed it.

In my early 30s, I lived in a hilltop cottage overlooking San Francisco Bay and created a small workshop for myself. It was an old gardening shed about seven feet square, with glass walls surrounded by giant redwood trees—and I loved it. It was there that I began "rehab thinking" to heal my attitude about my ability to create something original.

I embarked upon sculpting something in clay with the commitment to do so in one sitting, to never rework it, and to display it in my home in full view of visitors. On the one hand, this was scary; on the other, I experienced an unfamiliar feeling of relief that I'd set some parameters in advance. Having no idea what I was going to create but quite curious as to what would evolve, my hands prepared the clay. As I sat there on my stool asking for guidance, I went into a deep space, and with my eyes still closed, my hands began to move as if to become part of the clay.

As I slowly opened my eyes to see what was unfolding, my hands continued to intertwine with the clay. Before me was the naked figure of a woman lying limply on her back, outstretched over a rock. She was a victim, and she was dead. Stunned by what I saw, the meaning unfolded almost immediately, and I said aloud, "The victim is dead. I am this woman, and the victim in me is now dead." Simultaneously I began to laugh and cry at the gift of freedom from a victim consciousness that I'd just given myself . . . the gift of appreciating my fullest expression of what felt true for me.

Years later, our dearest friends, successful artists Andrea Smith and Matthew Smith (her son), invited Jerry and me to use their art studio in Lahaina, Maui. They had provided their own pastels and organized paper, tables, and so on for us to use for our sheer enjoyment. Although we were excited to get started, we found that we both had some judgments as to our limitations with respect to creating "something worthwhile." Remembering my powerful first experience with sculpting, I suggested that we use the same parameters and also frame or display whatever were the results of our unedited work.

We did so, with great encouragement from Andrea and Matthew. The turning point came when Andrea shared her philosophy that most people are creatively inhibited because there are so many preconceived rules as to what constitutes good versus bad art. She said, "It's amazing how many rules have been made up for filling a simple, blank piece of paper."

These experiences allowed us to create images and sculptures, some of which have been cast in bronze.

Creativity is a state of mind that can be
articulated in myriad ways. We're all artistic
but often allow fears and perceived limitations
to block the expression of our unique imaginations.
Freeing ourselves to create can help us define and give
form to the stages of growth on our spiritual journeys.

Avery's Passion for Life

— Jerry

While visiting Diane's relatives on the East Coast, we went for a walk with Avery, her four-year-old grandnephew.

His energy was focused on being fully and completely alive. His inner battery was superpowered, and while we were with him, it never ran out of juice. His bright eyes showed that he looked upon everything as fascinating and even beautiful. He was so happy to be alive that every pore of his body seemed to sing out, "What a great and gorgeous day this is!" Unlike the two of us, he wore no watch during our nature walk, and he frequently stopped or just meandered wherever his interest took him. He had no to-do list, no sense of rush, and no purpose other than enjoying the moment.

Throughout the walk, Avery's eyes sparkled and his enormous smile never wavered. He greeted everything he saw with enthusiasm, as if it were a new experience. While we were with him, there seemed to be no past or future, because he was so totally involved in the present. He exuded excitement about how wonderful it was just to breathe. At one point, he got on his knees to examine a weed and looked at it for a long time as if he were taking in every part of it to form a "heart print." Then he very gently pulled it out of ground, smelled it, tasted it, and then gave it to us to hold, saying with all the passion in his tiny being, "Isn't that the most beautiful thing you've ever seen?"

Spiritual teachers come in all sizes, some of them quite small. Young children remind us to bring passion and appreciation to each moment and to remember that the present is the only time we can consciously live in. Rushing through life to get to a future that will always be ahead of us or regretting a past that's over and can't be undone causes us to lose sight of <u>now,</u> which is the most important time in our lives.

$\mathcal{D}$o It Anyway!

— Diane

One of the great blessings of my life is that many of the people I knew as a child and adolescent are still in my life (and it's not as if we all grew up in the same town and remained there).

Living east of New York City on the more remote end of Long Island, the kids in my class came to school by train, bus, and car pool from more than a 50-mile radius. During 40 years of reunions, and some events in between, we've maintained our connections.

I believe that minds are joined at some level, and if we're open to this, communication between two people can occur without physical or auditory contact. This was never more apparent than on the eve of my birthday in 2005. During the night, I suddenly woke up—which is quite unusual for me—and decided to work at my computer. While reading a general e-mail from my high school classmates, the full image of a boy I knew in grade school suddenly came to mind. I hadn't seen him since we graduated high school, yet his image was surprisingly vivid.

Recalling the impression of him that I'd had as a girl of 10 or 11, I remembered a quiet, intelligent boy with a large build and mature sense of kindness, consideration, and compassion. At an early age, I knew what a special person he was.

Sitting at my computer, I felt guided to write him an e-mail expressing my experience of him. My ego quickly pushed that thought aside as ridiculous, yet the guidance persisted. Over the years, I've experienced the power of following my intuition, even when it seems to make no sense, so I found his e-mail address on the class roster and decided to write him anyway. The note was brief but included my appreciation for the kind of person he was as a young man and the impact he'd had on me.

"You were very much a kind and thoughtful friend in my life. Some things and people you never forget." I told him that I just wanted him to know that, and signed off the computer.

A number of weeks passed before I received a message back. It read:

> *I would have replied sooner to your e-mail of late, dated Feb. 2nd; however, I have been dealing with the death of my beloved wife. Early in the A.M. of Feb. 3rd, Jean suddenly passed. She was 55 yrs. old, and we were to celebrate our 35th wedding anniversary this April 4th.*

I was stunned by the news. We wrote back and forth and stayed in contact. I waited to see if other classmates knew about his wife's death, and when I didn't hear about it from anyone, I decided to let him tell them in his own time. Some months went by, and I received the thought that it was time to give the opportunity for a small group of male classmates to connect with and support our old friend. I wrote them and also included one of our female classmates, who at the time was a caregiver to her mother, who was nearing the end of a long and difficult struggle with Alzheimer's. They hadn't known each other well in our earlier years, but she reached out to support him, and he in turn comforted her through her mother's passing. They became good friends and eventually fell in love.

Whenever I doubt following my inner guidance, I remember these two and how their joining might never have occurred if I'd given in to my own reservations.

*We're musicians in a celestial orchestra,
each playing our small part to create the whole
symphony. But if we're afraid—if we doubt our
role—we'll never allow ourselves to play.*

Projection of Fear in Iran

— Jerry and Diane

In 1994, the head of oncology at Tehran's largest hospital invited us to lecture in Iran, which had no American embassy. We were aware that individuals who even unknowingly said the wrong thing could immediately be jailed there. Despite this, our guidance was to go and not be fearful. Many friends and relatives tried to dissuade us, saying that it was not only dangerous, but that the Iranian government was vehemently anti-American.

We arrived at our hotel at 3 A.M. and immediately noticed a huge banner that read: DOWN WITH AMERICANS. The night clerk informed us that we were the first Americans to stay there in 17 years, but he seemed extremely friendly and appreciative that we'd come. In fact, it appeared that most of the people we met had relatives in the U.S., and all of them were welcoming.

Our first lecture at the Cancer Institute was given in English to a packed auditorium of more than 500 people, with many others standing in the rear. Women sat on one side and men on the other. A few minutes before we began, our interpreter came up to us and pointed out a tall man in a black turban. She informed us that this man was from the government and would be listening carefully, taking notes about everything we discussed. She added, "Please be very careful what you say, because he'll be reporting back to his superiors."

As we began speaking, it was clear from the energy in the auditorium how much the audience was enjoying our talk. However, the man from the government was frowning and busily writing everything down. Later we compared our own mental notes and discovered that both of us had begun to fear that we'd end up in jail—the Attitudinal Healing principles we'd been talking about suddenly went out the window! After a few minutes of fear, however, it was as if we both made the same internal decision: to return to the principle that there are only two emotions—love and fear. Therefore, we had a choice: We could see this man as either loving or menacing. Since he didn't look loving, we'd both decided to see him as the latter. But rather than thinking of him as someone out to attack us, we now viewed him as someone who was afraid and asking for love.

Throughout the remainder of our lecture, we sent him caring thoughts, which allowed us to go back to a peaceful state of mind as we continued our talk and conducted a question-and-answer period after our formal presentation. Although we felt peaceful and centered, the man in the black turban continued to look angry as he frowned over his notes.

When the lecture was over, the chairman gave a ten-minute summary of our talk in Farsi, which is the primary language of Iran. A few moments later, the government man came up to us with his own translator. His eyes were soft and he was smiling. Through the interpreter, he told us that he had a confession to make: He didn't actually understand a word of English. But he said that after hearing the summary in Farsi, he was very pleased with our talk and would like to arrange other lectures while we were in Iran. To our amazement, he then asked to have his photograph taken with us!

When we project our own fears, we create frightening images within our surroundings, and that's what we see. Appearances can be, and often are, quite deceiving. A loving, peaceful mind looks beyond appearances to the oneness we share with all our brothers and sisters; thus, we see the situation at hand more accurately, because the perception now includes spiritual truth.

$\mathscr{S}$implicity in Tonga

— Jerry and Diane

We were invited to Tonga, an archipelago between Hawaii and New Zealand that has 169 islands, 36 of which are inhabited! One of the women we were working with on Tongatapu, the largest of them, was going to visit her mother on one of the distant islands and invited us to come along. We accepted, and this turned out to be a wise decision, because we learned several valuable spiritual lessons on our journey.

By our Western standards, her relatives were exceedingly poor, but even though they lacked financial wealth, their spirits were rich with love. Tey, our friend's mother, had obviously been planning for our arrival, because there was an amazing spread of food. Her family's hospitality, warmth, and kindness couldn't have been greater.

We learned that the people on this small island considered themselves to be a single family. If someone was injured or needed help, others treated that individual as if he or she were their own blood relation. There was no theft, because if someone needed something, it was provided; hence, there was no police force. The people of this island also related to nature as if every living thing deserved to be treated with love and respect.

The island had one public telephone that had broken down three years before our visit, and no one had bothered to repair it.

To us, this was paradise—no phones, no fax machines, and seemingly no one in a hurry. We were struck by how happy everybody was. Their lifestyle was quite simple, but it was imbued with love and caring for each member of the community.

When we returned home, we decided to find ways to bring more simplicity and balance to our lives. We've always been grateful to the people of that small island for showing us that it's possible to live as a single spiritual family when each member of the community treats others as he or she would like to be treated.

Imagine a life based on love and acceptance—one so simple that there's little to distract us from pursuing the deep values of the heart. Many people equate being busy with being important, but wouldn't all of our lives be richer if we valued loving and caring for each other more than acquisitiveness, accomplishment, and competition?

$\mathscr{P}$anic at the Opera House

— Diane

One of the first times Jerry and I lectured together was at the opera house in Seattle. We were backstage waiting to be announced, and Jerry looked through a peephole in the curtain. "Wow," he commented, "the house is packed."

This must have made him nervous because suddenly he expressed an overwhelming desire to urinate! Even though we knew that they were going to introduce us in a few minutes, he had to go, so he asked the stagehand where the bathroom was and raced toward it. Later, he told me that he ran as fast as he could, but as he started back, he realized that he'd exited from a different door into an adjoining building. He had to find his way back to the restroom and go out the correct door before he could locate me. He arrived just as we were being announced.

Meanwhile I was having my own anxieties. We'd only lectured together a few times, and I knew that people really came to hear Jerry. My anxiety quickly turned to anger. I said to myself, *I will never forgive Jerry for this*. Then I began fantasizing about what would happen if he didn't get back in time and the curtain rose and there I was, standing onstage alone. I decided that I'd tell the truth and say, "Sorry, Jerry went to the bathroom and he'll be right back."

We were out of the sight of the master of ceremonies as he began to introduce us. Just as he finished, Jerry came tearing across the stage with literally a second to spare. The curtain went up and we opened our lecture with the title of our talk, "Forgiveness Is the Key to Happiness!"

While onstage, I actually shared the fact that we were giving a talk on forgiveness, yet here I'd been just moments before thinking I'd "never" forgive Jerry, who was full of his own self-condemnation! Never more than that night did we recognize the truth of the old saying "You teach what you need to learn."

Awareness of the ego is essential if we're to attain a peaceful mind and a happy heart. Forgiveness requires us to look honestly at our thoughts and emotions and see how destructive judgment and anger are. Before we turn on the light, we have to see that it's dark.

Shopping Transformation

— Jerry

One of my least-favorite activities used to be shopping, by myself or with Diane. If I was alone, at least I could run in, get what I needed, and run out. And it's not as if Diane asked me to go with her that often—usually only around her birthday and Christmas. My problem was that after about a half hour, I'd get "antsy" and bored and wish that I were somewhere else.

A few years ago, I found a new way to approach shopping. During my morning meditation, I heard an inner voice instructing me that the next time I went I was to take a writing pad and pen and find a chair in the store where I could compose poetry and practice being close to Spirit.

When I go shopping with Diane now, I'm exactly where I want to be, filled with joy and completely patient. I don't even glance at my watch. On some occasions, Diane will even show me some clothes to get my opinion, and I remain a "happy camper."

A few months after we transformed our shopping experience, Diane was in a store with her mom. She was drawn to walk over to another department, not quite knowing why. As she entered the area, she noticed a young man sitting in a chair, looking angry and agitated as his wife was hurriedly sifting through rack of clothing.

Diane approached him, and after a few moments, she looked at him with a sympathetic smile and gently said, "This is tough, isn't it?"

Without missing a beat, he whispered, "I *hate* this. I can't stand being here."

Diane softly mentioned that her husband used to be that way, too—impatient and wanting to be someplace else. The young man caught the "used to" part and asked how her husband had turned it around.

Diane told him that I'd purposely decided to change my attitude and would now find a chair near where she was shopping and spend that time writing love poems to her. Just before we'd leave, Diane would sit down beside me and I'd lovingly read my poetry to her. We would consequently leave the store more in love than when we came in. The young man sat up straight and, a hopeful smile on his face, called out to his wife, "Honey, do you have a pen?"

On February 14, 2005, we hosted a Valentine's Day dinner at our residence in Kailua, Hawaii. Diane suggested that we all share something special about our relationships with our partners. That night I read a poem that I'd written for Diane a few years earlier in a department store:

Everything about you
Reminds me of God:

Your love for me
That continues to unfold,
Never stopping,
Always expanding.

No matter what my mood,
You continue to encompass me with your love
Through your eyes
Of continual acceptance,
Through your gentle touch and voice,
Through my always feeling safe in your arms;

You are truly
An angel sent to me
So I can be constantly
Reminded of the magnitude
Of God's Love.

You are the fresh air
Of the spring and a reflection
Of nature's beauty.

You are the
Sweetest music
In the universe;
You constantly remind me
Of who and what I am.

You open my heart
So that my love for you and God
Can be one and the same;
You are my
Teacher of Love and patience
And of nonjudgment
So I may experience
What love and gratitude
Are all about.

You have helped
Me experience
The power of
A sacred, holy bond
Where God always comes
First in our relationship.

I love you, Diane,
As I love God—
Totally, dearly, sweetly,
And eternally . . .

With all of my heart
Now,
Always,
And forevermore.

Thank you, Diane,
For being my forever valentine.

— *Jerry*

A situation doesn't have to be perfect to find peace and joy within it. No matter where we are, God is there with us, but we can't feel the Divine presence if we're angry, judgmental, impatient, or even mildly annoyed by circumstances.

When I First Knew

— Diane

I was about three and a half years old when I first knew with absolute certainty that there was something other than this reality. I may be unable to remember much of what happened between then and now, but I'll never forget the experience I had that day.

It happened without fanfare or outward influence, and I don't know what precipitated it. I only know that somehow it bridged the time before I was born and the present. I remember being acutely aware of what I was thinking and feeling. I was looking at my left hand and slowly rubbing my middle finger with my thumb.

A feeling of recognition and sadness came over me, followed by mild but distinct agitation, and I spoke out loud, "This is a trick. This is not really me." Feeling a bit miffed, I said aloud again, "Somebody stuffed me in here, and I'm going to have to stay for a long time." With that, I gave a big sigh of resignation and went out to play.

Part of the mystery of life is who we are, where we came from, and what we may have known on some level before we were born. Sooner or later, most of us have an experience that presents us with the possibility that we're really spiritual beings living for a temporary time in these bodies and personalities, which aren't our true identities.

My Dyslexia

— Jerry

I flunked kindergarten and had to repeat it. As a child, I thought of myself as stupid, and different from other kids—and it didn't help that my brothers were good students who picked everything up easily.

I had tremendous difficulty learning to read and spell; consequently, I was almost always in the bottom of my class academically. They put the dumb kids in the front row, so I always knew where *I* would be sitting. The front row was the home I didn't want to be in—it felt as if I were in a deep hole that I couldn't climb out of.

As a young boy, I believed that the amount of love you receive from your parents and teachers depended on how high or low your grades were. For many years I assumed a victim role and became stuck in it. My poor grades and learning difficulties made me believe that I was unlovable. I even blamed God for my troubles.

Because of this, my confusion about the way Home to God began early . . . and it didn't help that due to my dyslexia, I read the word *God* as "dog." As a child, I pictured Him as a giant of a man with a white, flowing beard and long white hair. I assumed that He would love me if I was good but would hurt and punish me if I was bad. I spent an amazing amount of time fearing God and waiting for some kind of punishment like a brick that might fall from the sky right on my head. Unfortunately, I carried many of these fears into my adulthood.

Because of the dyslexia, I've always had an extremely poor sense of direction. If someone instructed me to turn right at the second stoplight, I was quite likely to turn left. As a child—and even as an adult—I had repeated experiences feeling lost on my journey of life, of not being sure which direction to take. Often I found myself (literally and figuratively) going in a circle.

I spent my first 50 years on Earth either running away from God or believing there was no Higher Power. At 50, when I consciously began a spiritual journey, it was as if the rudder of my ship began finding its way Home to what I now know is a loving Creator.

For many of us, the early childhood experiences that inform how we interpret the world around us become a dark cloud that follows us wherever we go. The depth of our pain is often hidden, but it's always there.

It took me a long time to recognize that I could choose not to be a victim of the world I see. I now think of my dyslexia as a blessing that has allowed me to speak and write in a clearer, simpler, easy-to-understand way—to avoid the "gobbledygook" kind of language that only gets in the way of real communication. It also gave me more compassion for children who have learning problems and for their parents.

In some ways my dyslexia and the desire to discover more about that fearful child within motivated me to become a child psychiatrist. Later it inspired me to join with others in creating a multidisciplinary clinic, the Child Center, which was devoted to kids with learning challenges.

Many things that look like limitations and
disabilities can be perceived as blessings in disguise.

Not Good Enough

— Jerry

A major obstacle on my spiritual journey was growing up in a home that seemed to have a sign at the entrance asking: ARE YOU GOOD ENOUGH TODAY? Beneath this, the answer was written in huge letters: _NO!_

As a kid, I had many conversations with myself. Sometimes they were like a silent, repetitive mantra such as: "I can't do anything right." This negative feedback reinforced my already poor self-image. As a result, I felt sorry for myself and looked for reasons to compare myself with others, always coming out, of course, on the short end of the stick.

In preschool I wasn't good enough to carry a glass of water without spilling it or to walk without bumping into things. I couldn't pass kindergarten, was stuck at the bottom of my class through elementary school, and wasn't good enough at sports. I was consistently the last one chosen in sandlot baseball. I wanted to look like Charles Atlas, a guy with big muscles and lots of admiring girls. I believed that everyone who saw me would recognize that I wasn't good enough—for anything. I bought into that belief system and lived with it much of my life.

In 1949, when I was interning in Boston, I had an epiphany. The clumsiness of my childhood had followed me into my adult life, and I was dreading my upcoming rotation on the surgery ward. However, the head of surgery, Dr. Fishburn, liked me a lot and seemed confident in my abilities. In fact, I was the only intern he permitted to perform appendectomies and herniectomies that year; all the others just assisted. I found that I could actually be dexterous and, to my great surprise, had the potential to be an excellent surgeon.

Dr. Fishburn encouraged me to become one and was quite disappointed when he couldn't talk me into it. Even though I didn't choose surgery, I learned an important lesson about the difference between believing in myself—my real self—and continuing to buy into an old perception of who I was *failing* to be.

Perceiving ourselves as "not good enough" stunts our growth in the present, which has nothing to do with the past, and keeps us feeling limited and unfulfilled.

Our belief system affects everything we do. Doors open when we begin to have faith in ourselves. Because our minds are unlimited, nothing is impossible, and we're not bound by past perceptions of ourselves or others.

$\mathcal{M}$y Scotch Bottle

— Jerry

A bottle of Scotch was once my refuge. When I felt unloved and unlovable, Scotch on the rocks was the elixir that got rid of pain and depression and gave me a false sense of calmness and security. It numbed my guilt and self-condemnation. For me, alcoholism was a major detour that delayed any kind of spiritual awakening.

In 1973, after 20 years of marriage, I found myself divorced and consumed with guilt and anger. My life was fragmented, and my consumption of alcohol increased substantially. Not only was I poisoning myself, but my behavior and drinking were affecting my adult children and others who cared for me.

Alcohol was a place to temporarily hide—it helped me avoid facing my problems and fears—and although I felt absolutely hopeless, my atheism became more pronounced than ever. I believed with great certainty that there was no God.

In May 1975, when I was 50, Judith Skutch Whitson handed me the unpublished manuscript of *A Course in Miracles*. I asked her what it was about, and she replied, "God and spiritual transformation." I pointed out that she knew I was an atheist and wasn't interested in that sort of thing. She asked me to read just one page.

I consented, and had one of the most amazing experiences of my life. I heard a voice inside my heart say, *Physician, heal thyself. This is your way Home.* Then an indescribable feeling of peace and oneness with everything filled my entire being. With absolute certainty, I knew that I was going to change and live a life of service in which God's will and mine would be the same.

I became a student of the *Course* and began to work on the unhealed relationships I had with my ex-wife, my adult children, and others in my life, as well as with myself. The process of forgiveness became my heartbeat and my purpose. Shortly afterward, I helped establish the International Center for Attitudinal Healing. I also stopped drinking.

Many alcoholics live in a state of denial about their alcoholism. Part of the suffering they experience comes from denying the existence of something greater than themselves that can direct their lives and lead them to peace, happiness, and harmony.

Addiction to alcohol and its toxic effects on family life are one of society's most serious problems. Perhaps it's no accident that many individuals find Alcoholics Anonymous so beneficial—it's an organization that not only helps them put their Higher Power first, but also stresses the importance of forgiveness and admitting mistakes as keys to healing.

Bobby's Deathbed Wisdom

— Jerry

In 1976 I made a house visit to Bobby, a 14-year-old boy who was dying of cancer. He and his mother had attended group support sessions at our Center, but were no longer able to because his condition had worsened. Bobby and his mother had decided that he would die at home, and he seemed at peace with his coming death. When I came into his room, he lay pale and motionless, hooked up to a morphine drip to ease his pain. I sat down by his bed and held his hand in silence.

After about 30 minutes, a thought occurred to me and I shared it with him, even though I wasn't sure he could hear me. "Bobby," I said, "I have a tape recorder in my briefcase. You've been through an awful lot this past year. It seems to me that you could help other kids who have cancer by sharing your experiences and perhaps giving them some advice."

To my surprise, Bobby sat up and opened his eyes. He said, "Please give me the dictating machine." As he spoke, the blood came back into his face and his pallor disappeared. He talked for about ten minutes, and everything he said was important and helpful. But what I remember most was his statement: "Tell all those kids and adults you see to remember that their purpose in life—no matter what shape their body is in, and as long as they are breathing—*is to love and help others.*"

A week later Bobby died, but his spirit lives on through his tape, which continues to help thousands of people.

*When we're focused on assisting others, we
don't pay as much attention to our own bodies.
Loving and helping others is one of the greatest
gifts we can bestow upon the world and ourselves.*

Celestial Schedulers

— Diane

After my father died, I decided to travel for a while to see the world. In those days, most people hadn't flown, commercial jets were new, and working for the travel industry was very much the way to see new places. I interviewed with several airlines and decided that getting a job with TWA for the summer would be my objective.

En route to my final interview, I arrived at the Newark airport with one hour to spare before my departing flight. I entered the only café and sat in the only available seat—next to three men in business suits. It turned out that they ran TWA at Newark, and before leaving, they encouraged me to bid to be based there.

I laughingly responded, "I don't think so. I interviewed with TWA because I know that JFK Airport on Long Island is always 'open,' and I'm planning on living at home with my mother and brother." Newark was four hours away in traffic and therefore out of the question.

Life has its way with us, and sure enough, I was sent to Newark, New Jersey. Strangely enough, the only week that JFK was closed to new employee assignments in more than two years was the one in which *I* was assigned. That's less than a one percent chance of not getting what I wanted.

I was devastated and knew that my family would also be saddened. I remember calling my mother and crying while I shared the news that I wouldn't be living at home. She was stoic, reminding me to count my blessings for having a job and to trust that there was a larger plan for my life. Years later, I heard that after hanging up, she cried all afternoon.

Off I went to Newark—then considered the armpit of the airline industry. On my first training flight, the captain, Larry Girard, turned out to be one of the three men I'd met at the café. He was chief pilot over all flight crews and operations for TWA and was training someone that day.

Over the next few months, I learned to love my job and stayed on a bit longer to take advantage of the travel opportunities it offered. In addition, I connected with a nurse who worked with children with life-threatening illnesses, none of whom had even flown. Captain Girard and I collaborated on creating an opportunity for them to do so.

Later that year I invited my mom to visit me in New Jersey. Since she lived several hours away, I suggested that she stay over. I needed to stop at the airport for a few things and invited her to come to the office with me to meet the people I worked with. She declined, saying that she'd wait in the car. Something inside of me really wanted her to come in, and I kept encouraging her to do so, to the point of being pushy. She finally relented when I suggested that she could wait for me in the employee-lounge area.

She was introduced to a few people who worked there, and just before we left, I went into the central office to pick something up. There I ran into Captain Girard, who asked what I was up to. I mentioned that my mother was visiting, and we walked out together to meet her in the lounge. As we entered, she was sitting quietly across the room with her eyes downcast.

As Captain Girard looked down, she slowly looked up, before standing to greet us. I introduced them, and in the course of their conversation, they discovered that they'd both lost spouses of 25 years just two years before. They spoke of how challenging the upcoming holidays felt. Then there was a pause, and I remember standing between them, looking from one to the other, dazzled by what I realized was happening: They were falling in love at first sight. The following August they were married, and the rest is 36 years of family history!

They were always convinced that I planned it all, but I insist on crediting "Celestial Schedulers." I was privileged to witness their first hellos and their last moments of saying good-bye. Larry Girard, a beautiful man and stepfather to me, passed away in the early-morning hours of July 25, 2003, as Mom and I held his hand and released him on his road back Home.

What appear to be adversities are often our best signposts in finding our way Home. Holding a place for gratitude when, amid life's twists and turns, the journey deviates from our well-laid plans, allows us to honor a Plan that's much greater than our own.

Jessica's Wisdom

— Jerry

We were lecturing in Aspen, Colorado, and a dear friend who lived there kindly offered us his home since he was going to be away. One afternoon as we were lying out in the yard, Jessica, the house manager's six-year-old daughter, came over for a visit. To my surprise, I found myself asking her a question that seemed completely inappropriate for a child her age.

"Why do you think we're here on Earth, and what do you think our purpose here is?"

Looking at me with raised eyebrows, Diane let me know that she also thought that was a pretty intense question for a child. Then, to our astonishment, Jessica began answering in a simple yet profound way.

"Oh, I think that when you come here, you come to help others and to love all things, even the earth and the trees. And when you die, I think that you should leave the earth a better place than when you got here." We were amazed at the old wisdom coming from a girl who lived alone with her mother in a one-room log cabin in the woods.

Diane: "Those are wonderful thoughts, Jessica. Did you learn them from your parents?"
Jessica: "No."

Diane: "Did you learn them at school?"

Jessica: "No. I don't go to school."

Diane: "What about Sunday school—did you learn about them there?"

Jessica: "No. I don't go there either."

Diane: "Well, Jessica, please tell us where you learned them."

Jessica: "Oh, I knew about all those things before I came here . . . you know . . . before I was born."

Because children are such wise spirits, it's
important to truly take the time to listen to them.
Imagine what a wonderful world this would be if
we simply practiced helping and loving each other
and working to make the earth a better place to live.

A Friend and a Teacher

— Jerry

I met Arnold Beisser when I was a first-year student at Stanford University School of Medicine. We were roommates throughout medical school. At the time, I didn't realize that we would remain lifelong friends or that he would help me learn what friendship was really about.

Arnie had a wonderful sense of humor and was extremely athletic. As a tennis player, he was ranked eighth in the country. In 1949, we graduated from medical school. He hoped to be a surgeon, and I wanted to be a psychiatrist. About a week after graduation and just before starting his internship, Arnie became ill. Even before entering the hospital, he correctly diagnosed himself as having polio.

I flew to see him, and found that he was in an iron lung in critical condition. None of the physicians expected him to live, but they didn't know what a fighter Arnie was and that he didn't believe in the word *impossible*. He pulled through but remained a quadriplegic, completely dependent on others for the rest of his life. It would have been easy, even understandable, for him to become bitter and angry about what seemed like a cruel twist of fate for someone so athletic and gifted. Adding to the irony was the fact that he contracted the poliovirus shortly before the Salk vaccine was introduced.

While Arnie did put his tennis trophies in the garage and lost interest in sports for some time, he later wrote *The Madness in Sports,* which was published in 1967. After that, he brought his trophies back into his living room.

I remember that he told me, "When people ask me how I feel about being restricted to a wheelchair, I answer, 'I don't choose to respond to that, because it's a limiting question. But if you want to ask me all the things I can *do* in a wheelchair, I'll be happy to answer you.'" Later in life, Arnie wrote a beautiful book called *Flying Without Wings,* which has been inspirational to so many people. It details his experiences with polio and physical dependence on others and is invaluable for those dealing with a disability.

Despite his paralysis, Arnie managed to give me so much more than I thought I could ever give him. He taught me and thousands of others how to go through life with a positive attitude regardless of what happens to our bodies.

Arnie and his occupational therapist, Rita, fell in love and married. Later, he took a residency in psychiatry and became head of the Metropolitan State Hospital, which was perhaps the most "dysfunctional" mental institution in California. Arnie transformed it into one of the state's best hospitals.

Years later, he told me that he was resigning from the hospital. "I need a new challenge," he explained. After all he'd been through, it was difficult for me to believe that he needed a *new* challenge, but he became the director of the Los Angeles County Department of Mental Health, a most demanding job, and he also assumed a full professorship at UCLA.

While Arnie didn't profess to be religious, there was a Light in him that was obvious to everyone. People were affected by his quiet spirituality, even if he didn't have a name for it.

When I first started on *my* spiritual pathway in 1975, Arnie was skeptical about what I was doing and felt that I might be ridiculed by my medical colleagues. Years later, I was giving a lecture at UCLA, and he sat in the audience, showering me with his complete approval and love.

Until he died at age 65, hardly a day went by that Arnie and I didn't talk on the phone. He seemed to get a vicarious thrill when I called him from such places as China, Russia, Thailand, India, Argentina, Australia, Ghana, New Zealand, and the many other countries I visited. It was as if my longtime friend was traveling with me wherever I went. Our friendship nourished us both to depths that I'd never thought possible. Without knowing it, Arnie became my greatest teacher.

There was nothing we couldn't tell each other because we knew that we wouldn't be judged by the other person. He taught me the power of humor and hope in the healing process, and that when you're helping another—which he spent his life doing—you're also helping yourself. Above all, Arnie taught me that the only thing that really matters in life is love.

He also showed me how to look beyond the physical. When he first became ill, all I could see was a withered, paralyzed body that was in extreme pain. When I visited him, initially it was difficult for me to see him in this condition. As time passed, though, I learned to look beyond his body and see the real Arnie, who always remained full of compassion and love for others.

Although we both felt free to say anything that was on our minds, perhaps the most important aspect of our relationship was expressed by the silence of our love and appreciation, the softness we could see in each other's eyes, and the knowledge that we would always be there for one another. Sometimes love is most powerful in those silent moments spent with another where words are not only unnecessary, but actually get in the way.

A few months after Arnie's death, Rita was visiting Diane and me. We took a walk and passed by a beautiful grove of trees. Rita paused and then said, "Arnie is in my car—I mean, his ashes are in my car. I take them with me wherever I go, looking for a place to scatter them. Would it be all right if we scattered his ashes here at the base of these trees?" Of course we said yes, and every day when we took our morning walk over the hills and by the trees, we'd stop and say, "Good morning, Arnie."

*Deep friendship is the home of love, trust, honesty, faith,
and the freedom to be ourselves at our craziest moments,
yet still know that we'll be accepted and loved as we are.*

To Give Is to Receive

— Diane

Jerry and I were just leaving for the airport after a workshop in Dallas when a well-dressed woman approached, stopping about eight feet from me. After finishing my conversation with our hosts, I turned to inquire if she wanted to speak to me. She shook her head but continued to stand there staring at me.

After a few minutes, I once again inquired if she had anything to ask me, as we were going to be leaving quite soon. Yet again her body language implied *no*, but something else was saying *yes*. At that point, Jerry and our hosts stated that we'd have to leave immediately if we were to catch our flight.

As I turned to get into the car, an internal voice told me to give her a copy of the *Mini Course,* which I'd referred to in the workshop. I took the little booklet out of my pocket, went over to her, and once again heard a voice from inside, this time telling me to offer her my phone number. "My guidance is to give this to you, and I'm also putting my phone number here. If you decide that you want to talk, please feel free to call me."

Two days later, she called and told me that for over a year she'd been greatly distressed because her newly married daughter, who was living nearby at the time, was raped during a forced entry into her home. The mother added that because she'd been unable to free herself from this extreme trauma, her daughter and son-in-law had finally moved to Boston in order to heal, saying that it was too difficult to deal with their own pain when hers was so great. Needless to say, the mother was doubly devastated.

She asked if I could help, and I suggested that we both do the 18-day *Mini Course* that I'd given her. She agreed, and we embarked on a journey of daily 15-minute calls. Each morning we discussed how we experienced the previous day's lesson and then took turns reading the new one for the day. Not surprisingly, the lessons I did were ideally suited to the different situations that presented themselves. Partway into this commitment, I realized that what I'd offered her was exactly what I needed myself.

Near the end of the second week, we realized that the 18th lesson was going to fall on Christmas morning. When that day arrived, she called me at the appointed time and shared that she'd recently been talking with her daughter about the many new ways she was learning to see and deal with the incident. She also reported that early that morning the doorbell had rung, and much to her surprise, it was her daughter and son-in-law. They'd been so moved by her growth and by the positive changes she'd been making that they'd decided not only to fly in to visit, but also to move back to Dallas to be near her again.

*One of the Principles of Attitudinal Healing
that brings us back to our center is that giving and
receiving are the same. Because we are one, when we give to
another, we give to ourselves. But we also do much more:
We strengthen our faith in connection and love.*

Miracles in Belfast

— Jerry and Diane

In the mid-1980s, we were invited to give a lecture and consult with various individuals in Belfast, Northern Ireland. This was a time of great hardship, high unemployment, and sectarian violence. Streets were cordoned off, and evidence of recent bombings was everywhere.

We'd been asked to meet with a family whose 14-year-old son, Billy, had muscular dystrophy. He was depressed because the week before, his best friend, who had the same disease, had died. (Muscular dystrophy is hereditary, and most children who have it die during their teenage years.)

When we arrived at Billy's home, his parents pointed to a nearby house where a bomb had killed three people a few days before. We spent about an hour with Billy, who was confined to a wheelchair. Before leaving, we asked him, "If a miracle occurred and you could be granted any wish, what would it be?" Without hesitating, he replied, "I would like to fly in a helicopter."

Later that afternoon, we called the airport to find out about the possibility of renting one. The man who answered asked us where we were from. When we said "the United States," he responded, "Well, this isn't the United States. You're in Belfast, and it's impossible to rent a helicopter here." We asked if any corporate helicopters landed there. He replied that they did, that one was there now in fact, and that the pilot was having coffee. He asked if we'd like to talk to him.

We told the pilot about Billy's wish and asked if he could ride in the company's helicopter. His immediate response was that it would be impossible because permission would have to come from the president of the company and he'd never allow it.

We inquired if the pilot believed in miracles, to which he replied, "Not that kind." Refusing to give up, we then asked him for the phone number of his company's headquarters. He gave it to us, but added that we were wasting our time.

Since we believe that nothing is impossible if we don't put limits on our minds, we dialed the number. The president's secretary was out, and he himself answered. After we shared Billy's story, he became quite enthusiastic about helping. He said, "Have that boy at the airport at 5 tomorrow afternoon, and the pilot will give him the ride of his life."

The next day, we discovered that the helicopter was quite large, with room for other passengers. Billy invited two of his friends, his sister, and a neighbor who'd never flown before. At 5 P.M., Billy and a cavalcade of cars, ours included, entered the airport. It was a spectacular day, and Billy did indeed have the ride of his life.

While in Belfast, we also met a blind man who had started a school that included both Protestant and Catholic children in the same classrooms. He told us that he was showing these kids that people of different faiths don't have horns sticking out of their heads. He taught them how to live and work with each other in harmony.

We asked him how long he'd been without sight, and he told us that he was now 40 and had been blind since someone threw a bomb into his house when he was 14. He added, "I believe that every negative circumstance can be turned into a positive. I wouldn't be doing the work I'm doing if I hadn't had that experience. I discovered that there's another kind of vision—*spiritual* vision. I decided to see everyone through Christ's eyes and spend what time I had left making forgiveness and love my way of life."

Needless to say, our time in Belfast enriched our faith in miracles and in the power of forgiveness.

Within any circumstance, we can be
open to hope and miracles in our lives.

Fear Before Surgery

— Jerry

Several years ago I was scheduled for glaucoma surgery on my right eye. Since my left one is legally blind from glaucoma, I found myself asking, *What happens if the surgery isn't a success and I end up being totally blind?*

That question didn't make me feel peaceful, so I reminded myself that by remaining stuck in fear of a future I couldn't control, I wasn't using Attitudinal Healing principles. So I decided to stay in the present and not raise questions about my future. I did my best in this regard by attempting to be helpful to others in any way I could.

Before leaving for the hospital, I meditated, so I felt quite peaceful when Diane and I arrived that morning. The nurse in the preoperative room seemed very surprised to find me so tranquil and remarked that my heart rate wasn't rapid like most other surgical candidates. She asked what I did to be so calm.

I explained my meditation technique to her and told her about my close relationship with God. The nurse said, "I'm having a lot of trouble with my faith today. Please tell me in more detail about your relationship with God." I talked to her about how I try to devote my life to God and to others each day.

The nurse left to attend to another patient, then returned to sit by my side until well after her shift had ended. She said, "Please tell me more about how you experience God." I told her that when I acknowledge being surrounded by the love of the Creator, there's nothing to fear, and I can safely put the future in His hands. We talked until the anesthesiologist came in.

I knew of one way I could stay in the present with this new arrival. Anesthesiologists were having challenges with HMOs because of the reduced amount of money they were paying out, so I asked him how this was affecting him personally. He described in great detail his feelings of hurt, disappointment, and anger about what was happening. Afterward, he sighed with relief at being able to vent about those painful issues. Looking at me, he said, "Thank you for asking. . . . Well, let's get on with our business here."

Then they rolled me into surgery. I knew that my surgeon was a close friend of my brother Art, who was a famous ophthalmologist. I told her that if I were in her shoes, I would feel him looking over my shoulder, letting me know that I'd better not make any mistakes! She laughingly agreed. I also told her that I sensed it would be better for both of us if, during the surgery, she thought of me as just Jerry Smith and not Dr. Jerry Jampolsky, brother of Dr. Arthur Jampolsky. She flashed a big smile of relief and nodded her head in agreement. The entire surgical experience—not just the procedure itself—was a huge success!

Egos love to worry about future events, particularly
those that contain an element of risk. And worry leads
to deeper fears—which, in turn, lead to more worry. Concentrating
on being caring allows us to remain in the present, where
the Source of Love also resides in our hearts.

A Shift in Perception

— Diane

About two years after Jerry underwent glaucoma surgery, he had another challenge that involved his vision when he developed a severe eye infection. He had previously lost 90 percent of the sight in his left eye, and the right was now threatened with complete blindness due to an infection inside his eyeball. Antibiotics were administered by inserting a needle into it, but this didn't appear to be helping, and another dangerous procedure was presented as the only hope for saving his vision. Unfortunately, a less-than-desirable outcome was also predicted.

His doctors, the best in their field, saw no other recourse than surgery, so Jerry was immediately scheduled for a pre-op procedure and exam meeting at the University of California, San Francisco. Since I was then doing postdoctoral work at the same UCSF campus, I needed to be in the city earlier that day and drove separately. Sally Kinn, one of the first children at our Center who survived leukemia, and who was turning 40 that day, chauffeured Jerry.

When we found out that it was a milestone birthday, I asked her why she wasn't spending such an important day having fun with the meaningful people in her life. She replied that she never expected to live to see 40 and couldn't think of anyone else she'd rather spend her birthday with than Jerry. She was happy to help because of all he'd done for her. Needless to say, an angel escorted him that day.

Driving across the Golden Gate Bridge on this beautiful, sunny day, I decided to "have a conversation" with Mother Teresa and Sister Sylvia, both of whom had recently died and who had been very close to each other and to us. Visualizing them, I said, "If Jerry is going to be blind for the rest of his life, I accept that. If, on the other hand, we're blocking his healing, please guide us to release this in any way that's appropriate." I was then guided to ask, "If it's in Divine Order, could you please dissolve 50 percent of Jerry's eye infection to avoid the operation scheduled for tomorrow?"

Prior to the exam, we met in the outer office, and I recounted my "conversation" on the bridge to Jerry and Sally. He smiled and said, "Let's expect a miracle!"

The surgeon conducting the pre-op exam dimmed the lights in the room to better see through his lenses. Just after moving in to take a look, he literally jumped back. "We must have made some mistake: Your eye is a good 50 percent less infected than yesterday! What did you do between then and now?" he excitedly asked.

I told him about my "conversation" on the bridge. He just stared at Jerry, then at me, and finally said, "Well, I want to postpone the operation and have you come in again tomorrow so I can have a look at this. And by the way, whatever you did in your 'conversation' today, do it again before tomorrow's appointment."

The next day we were again driving in separate cars. Once more, midway over the Golden Gate Bridge, I began my "conversation." This time I thanked both Mother Teresa and Sister Sylvia for their help in decreasing Jerry's infection and asked that, if doing so was in Divine Order, they clear up the other 50 percent. If not, we'd completely accept the alternative.

The surgeon approached Jerry's eyes more cautiously, obviously remembering his surprise at the previous day's results. This time, he pushed himself back from the table and rolled his chair toward me. With a slow, metered cadence he said, "The infection is gone. There's no need to operate now. I've never seen this before. What happened here?"

We told him about my second "conversation" and asked if he had any other explanation for this complete remission. He said that he had none. We then asked him if he believed in miracles, and he replied, "Maybe I had better!"

Advanced glaucoma is a serious degenerative disease that usually leads to blindness. Both of Jerry's parents lived into their 90s and were blind, one from glaucoma and the other from macular degeneration. It's many years later now, and Jerry's eyes have remained essentially the same.

"Miracles are a natural occurrence when we are willing to shift our perceptions to remove the blocks to the awareness of love's Presence in our lives." — *A Course in Miracles*

The Healing Power of Laughter

— Jerry and Diane

For a number of years, we participated as keynote speakers in "The Healing Power of Laughter and Play" conferences in many U.S. cities. We were always met at the airport gate by a group of outrageously dressed clowns. Even after a long flight, this always cheered us up and ensured that we would be in a great mood. Bringing additional spontaneity to these already-unpredictable events was the participation of some great "old time" comedians such as Red Skelton and Steve Allen.

During a conference in Florida, we met an individual who helped us shift our perceptions about financial difficulties. At one point during the lecture, we asked if any of the clowns in attendance wanted to share how they'd gotten where they were today. Many of them spoke up to recount some amazing stories, but one in particular touched us deeply.

An especially talented clown began his story and soon had everyone's rapt attention. He had been a financially successful commodities trader on Wall Street until the 1980s stock-market crash when he lost everything. Deciding to seriously reevaluate the purpose of his life, he asked himself for the first time, *What do I really want to do with my life? What would make me happy?* The answer he received was quite a surprise. Rather than attempt to rebuild his material fortune, a little voice advised him, *Be a clown!*

He was shocked . . . until he remembered that long before financial ambitions had ruled his life, that's exactly what he'd wanted to be. So off to clown school he went, and here he was. He ended by stating that while he didn't have material riches, he was "the wealthiest, happiest man alive."

To give love and laughter is to claim them for ourselves. Money, material possessions, and power don't necessarily bring lasting happiness. Laughing is a wonderful elixir that allows us to heal ourselves.

$\mathcal{T}$eachers of Love

— Jerry and Diane

Our longtime friends Jack and Eulalia Luckett, who live in Waikiki, Hawaii, are two of the most nonjudgmental and joyous people we've every known. We think of them as urban monks, although they're very much involved in the world. They always have time to help those who need a moment of encouragement and hope.

While they've been on a spiritual path for many years, they don't belong to any religious organizations; rather, they simply devote themselves to spreading love and happiness to whomever they meet. Both of them have also endured their fair share of trauma, so their decision to live lives devoted to giving has been consciously made.

Eulalia was one of the first women to graduate from Harvard with an M.B.A. Jack was a lawyer, formerly a district attorney, who'd been a colonel in the Marines and had fought and nearly died in both Korea and Vietnam. He was also the executive director of the International Center for Attitudinal Healing in the early years when it was located in Tiburon.

Wherever she goes, Eulalia always has a sheet of small colored hearts in her purse. When she's at a restaurant, she asks the waitperson's name and favorite color and then presents him or her with a brightly colored heart. Invariably, love begins to flow around the table.

Jack and Eulalia laugh a lot and don't take themselves too seriously. People feel good and joyful in their presence. They truly live in a consciousness of giving and caring for others. We've asked ourselves how they can be so consistently lighthearted and have concluded that it's because they do a wonderful job of holding no grievances. We've never heard them say a negative word about anyone.

They also live quite simply and have given away most of their possessions. Money and material objects have never been their "god." Their lives demonstrate their absolute commitment to surrendering to love. Their path is straight and leads to peace. They never "pontificate" or try to change other people's beliefs or attitudes. Yet, because they practice unconditional love, they demonstrate the joy and peace of the Sacred. Their compassion and generosity of spirit can't help but inspire those around them.

To actively walk the path of love—and to
do so lightly, with eyes soft and full of light—
is to give the world a precious gift.

Believing in Miracles

— Jerry

I had always been a great admirer of Mother Teresa and hoped that one day I'd be able to meet her. Because a good friend knew the priest who was in charge of arranging her schedule when she was in the U.S., I got on the list of those who would be allowed to make her acquaintance.

Since I was due to lecture in New York City, it was arranged for me to see her there the following Sunday. Friday evening, however, I received a call from the parents of a child whose cancer had taken a critical turn for the worse. Since he was only expected to live a day or two, they asked if I'd fly back to be with him and the family. I canceled my meeting with Mother Teresa and was told that the next time she came to the U.S., another one would be arranged.

About a year later, I was informed that a 20-minute interview with Mother Teresa over the Fourth of July weekend in Los Angeles had been scheduled. Our meeting actually lasted for an hour and changed my life. Just being in her presence brought me an incredible sense of peace. I told her that I'd like her help in learning how to surrender to love and to God.

I'd been informed that Mother Teresa was going to fly to Mexico City the following day. Since I had no pressing obligations, I said, "Mother, I'm finding so much peace being in your presence, could I fly to Mexico City just to spend more time with you?"

She looked gently into my eyes and said, "Dr. Jerry, I have no objection, and it would be all right if you want to come." My heart leapt with a silent *Yippee!* But after a few seconds, she added, "You say that you've come to me to learn more about total surrender. I believe you would learn more about it if instead of going to Mexico, you gave the money it would cost to fly there to the poor."

I wasn't prepared for the depth of the lesson I received that day. I flew back to San Francisco and donated the amount of the flight to the Missionaries of Charity. Mother Teresa taught me that true healing takes place in the present. When I let go of my need to see her again and gave that money to the poor, a sense of peace and a sweetness such as I'd never experienced before came over me.

After her return to Calcutta, I dictated a letter to Mother Teresa thanking her for the gift of knowledge she had given me. To my amazement, six weeks later I received a handwritten response, and we began a correspondence that made me feel so blessed.

Many years later I was on a lecture tour that included Bombay, India. I had taken my son Lee with me. The organizers knew that I was acquainted with Mother Teresa and asked if I would pick her up at the house of the Missionaries of Charity and bring her to the conference, where she was scheduled to speak.

Lee and I had been conflicted about whether to give money to the children with no fingers who begged at stop signs and came up to our taxi. We worried that doing so might encourage parents to cut off their children's fingers. While driving to the conference with Mother Teresa, we asked her how she approached this problem. She replied, "The rumors of some parents cutting off their children's fingers are true, so I just bless them and send blessings to their parents."

There was a large press conference for Mother Teresa, which she asked me to conduct—something I'd never done before. Immediately afterward, she was scheduled to leave for lectures at a variety of locations, and a small caravan of vehicles arrived to accompany her: A physician and some other dignitaries were in the first car, there was a van filled with nuns, and Mother Teresa got into the middle car.

As Lee and I were saying good-bye, she asked, "Would you and your son like to join me as I travel and give my talks?" We both gave her an immediate "Yes!"

At one point during our journey, Lee said that he had a tape recorder and asked if he might interview her. She replied that that would be fine. One of the questions he asked was: "I'm about to get my Ph.D. in psychology. What are the most important traits people should have when they go into the healing professions?"

"Humility and meekness," she replied.

I couldn't resist responding, "Mother, they don't teach those in professional schools in the United States."

Later we arrived at a town where 3,000 people had gathered, but since there were no police present, Lee and I ended up protecting Mother Teresa and leading her through the crowd to the podium.

After we returned home, it was hard for us to realize that we'd actually spent nine hours in the same car with Mother Teresa. When people ask me if I really believe in miracles, my response is always quick: "I sure do!"

There are no coincidences. When we become completely unattached to the outcome, new doors will open. It's in letting go that we receive; it's in giving that we gain.

A Gift of Sugar

— Jerry and Diane

While visiting with Mother Teresa outside Rome, sitting among the ruins of an ancient church, we talked for many hours. During that time, she related an experience she'd recently had in Calcutta, India.

She told us about a little boy, approximately six years old, who was from the same poverty-stricken neighborhood where she and many other Sisters lived and worked. He had heard about Mother Teresa and the Missionaries of Charity and wanted to help them in some way.

Early one morning, the little boy approached her. Before speaking, he looked up at her and slowly opened his hand to expose a little pile of sugar. In his small, clear voice, he said, "Mother, I heard you had no sugar." He'd saved his ration and wanted to give it to people who needed it more than he did.

With tears in her eyes, Mother told us, "You know, people give truckloads of gifts and supplies to help support our work, and we're always so grateful. But with the gift of a handful of sugar, this little child made me realize more profoundly than ever that *it is not how much we give in life that really counts. What is more important is how much _love_ we give it with.*"

Whenever we're tempted to measure or judge ourselves for what we have or haven't done, we remember Mother Teresa's words, and we now use them as a guiding light for our lives.

When we make an offering from the heart, there are no strings and no expectations. To truly give is to seek nothing in return because we're expressing love, which is the greatest gift in the world.

Shoe Inserts

— Jerry

A few years ago I found myself hanging on to anger toward—and disappointment in—myself. Even though I'd written a book on forgiveness, I was having trouble forgiving myself. One night I went to bed and asked the universe for help.

In the middle of the night, I woke up with an inspired thought: I was to make a small insert that would fit inside my shoe. It would read: "May every step you take be one of forgiveness."

If this could be helpful to me, I assumed that it could also be so to others. I designed a foot-shaped insert with the forgiveness statement and the Website of the Center on it. We tell people that each step they take while wearing one will not only remind them to forgive, but will help heal their soul.

May
  Every
    Step
      You
        Take
  Be One Of
  Forgiveness

Through the years, the shoe inserts have been translated into many languages, with tens of thousands having been given away. When we're at restaurants, we often give one to the waitstaff and tell them that if somebody gives them a hard time, it will remind them to forgive and put a smile back on their face.

When we're asked to remove our shoes at airports, we show the inserts to the security agents, who frequently laugh and ask for one. An agent once said, "I don't think *I* need one, but my wife sure does!"

We need all the help we can get to remind us
that forgiveness is as important as breathing.

*A*ttitudinal Healing and the Police

— Jerry and Diane

In May 2005 we were invited by the Center for Attitudinal Healing in Brazil to lecture and give workshops in São Paulo and Brasília. We were given little information about our talk except that off-duty police officers would be attending on a volunteer basis. To be honest, we were leery of how receptive these individuals would be to our message, but we let go of our doubts and trusted our inner guidance to lead the way. We also released any attachment to the results.

With a metropolitan population of more than 18 million, São Paulo is one of the largest cities in the world. Like other huge urban areas, it has many positive attributes but is also beset by violence, drug use, and a large number of homeless people. Our hosts, Luiz and Rita Pontes of the Brazilian Center for Attitudinal Healing, didn't expect more than 20 to 40 officers to attend. To everyone's surprise, over 300 showed up, many of them just off their beats—all wearing bulletproof vests and armed with handguns.

Before we spoke, we met with the colonel who was in charge of the 3,500-member police force working in the southern district of the city. He said that he was intrigued by the subject of our talk, "Attitudinal Healing in the Police Department," and would be attending. We gave him one of our forgiveness shoe inserts, and he liked it so much that he immediately put it in his shoe.

We talked about the importance of the role of the police in protecting external society—and how well they'd learned to fulfill it—adding that unfortunately, they were often far less successful at protecting the internal "society" of their families' lives and their own. While often hidden, domestic violence, alcohol and drug abuse, and divorce are actually quite high in law-enforcement families. We discussed how the application of the Principles of Attitudinal Healing offers another way of looking at attack and defense—and, ultimately, of viewing their often-shadowy world.

During the discussion part of our presentation, there were two officers who'd attended an Attitudinal Healing Support Group at the Center in their city. One stated that in the marines, he'd been taught to hate and kill, and that this outlook had been reinforced when he joined the police. Through Attitudinal Healing, he said that he'd begun to look at the world differently—to see the fear in the heart of the person behind the offense.

A female officer who had attended the Attitudinal Healing Support Group said that she'd taken a leave of absence from the department because of an issue with her superior. She, too, found that the group helped her see things differently. She practiced forgiveness, returned to her job, and now had a harmonious relationship with the same superior.

When we finished, the colonel told us that Attitudinal Healing was the paradigm they'd been waiting for. He expressed a desire to have Luiz and Rita offer expanded in-service training for their entire department. He also requested 3,500 shoe inserts in Portuguese!

*No matter what type of work we do, forgiveness can
play an important function in how we conduct our lives.*

The AIDS Poster

— Jerry and Diane

In 1985 we lectured at the United Nations headquarters in Santiago, Chile, surrounded by the sea and majestic snowcapped mountains. During our visit, we were taken to one of the city's hospitals, where we met the chief pediatric oncologist.

He told us that they'd just admitted their first child with AIDS, adding that his staff—as well as the general public—were ill informed about how people become infected and were fearful that they might contract the disease. He asked if we had any ideas about how to correct their misperceptions.

"Since Chile is primarily a patriarchal society," we said, "people will tend to accept *your* actions. We suggest that you hold a press conference with all the media—newspapers, magazines, radio, and television. Then have them take a photo of you hugging this child. That photo will teach more powerfully than words that you can't get infected with AIDS by hugging or touching."

He wrote us later to tell us that he'd done as we suggested and it had been successful. Since confusion and fear about how AIDS is transmitted wasn't limited to Chile, we recognized that we needed to do something more to help alter public opinion about children with the virus. We wanted to create an image that would say it all at a glance, since that's just about the only chance there is of getting someone's attention. But how to include the most important messages in just one image was the challenge.

After meditating and asking for guidance, we knew that we wanted to put a face on AIDS that would open people's hearts while also addressing the psychological and social needs of those who were increasingly being isolated from society by this disease. In addition, we wanted to educate people that AIDS isn't contagious through everyday, casual contact. We needed a single image that would cross all cultural divisions. While we knew what we wanted to convey, we hadn't a clue as to what the finished product should look like.

It occurred to us that Jack Keeler—the creator of Granny Goose and other logos, who also did the drawings and cover images for three of our books, *Love Is Letting Go of Fear, Love Is the Answer,* and (for children) *Me First and the Gimme Gimmes*—might be able to help.

However, when we first approached Jack with our need, he balked at the idea. "I'm a cartoonist. I do cartoons that are funny, and there's nothing humorous about a child having AIDS." We told him that we weren't asking for something humorous, but rather for an educational image that would go straight to people's hearts. Jack replied, "I wouldn't know how to do that."

We explained that we knew he didn't know—and that that was okay. We said that we also knew that he was ambivalent about turning to God for help, but we suggested that he nevertheless do so. Jack replied, "Okay, I'll try . . . but I don't think it will work."

A week later, he came to us with a single sheet on a drawing board. There it was—complete perfection in one image. It was an illustration of a child standing in a field of flowers, arms outstretched, with the following legend: "I have AIDS. . . . Please hug me. . . . I can't make you sick."

It was perfect, and so simple that we cried with joy and gratitude. In our minds, Jack had really stepped aside and let God lead him as he drew this cartoon.

In 1987, we printed the drawing as a poster and included the Center's information and the phone number for the first AIDS hotline in the country for kids, staffed by the Center. It became the most widely distributed AIDS poster in the world and was adopted by the World Health Organization in Geneva, who named it one of the most effective international AIDS educational tools to date. It has been reproduced in numerous languages and distributed to 140 countries. It was also given out free to all who asked and was made available for duplication to organizations naming their own local support networks.

The AIDS hotline became an educational resource for adults, teens, and kids, as well as for educators and religious leaders. One of our goals with the hotline was to have a place where hemophiliacs who might have contracted the AIDS virus in the country's then-tainted blood supply could come out of hiding and get much-needed support. It worked, and many hospitals later instituted their own hotlines.

The most inspirational ideas are also often the simplest.
Love isn't complex unless we choose to make it so.

A Healing Story

— Jerry

I was visiting Patsy Robinson—a dear friend since the early days of the Centers for Attitudinal Healing, of which she was a founder—in her home. She is now deceased. At the time, she was having severe medical difficulties, was suffering from lung problems, and was on constant oxygen. She also had a grievance toward a man she considered a friend who had betrayed her financially. She'd tried to forgive him but hadn't succeeded.

Since she was asking for my help, I shared some of my experiences of letting money and what I thought was "fair" interfere with my peace of mind and my spiritual journey. I mentioned that writing a letter often helps release both parties.

A few days later, she e-mailed me a copy of the letter she'd sent to this man. I found it to be such a powerful model for letting go, being honest, and creating an atmosphere conducive to releasing the past that I wanted to share it. Naturally, the man's name has been omitted.

July 29, 2004

Yesterday I had a long talk with Jerry Jampolsky. Our discussion was about forgiveness and how important it is in our lives in order to move on and be peaceful. That is something that is very important for me to do right now. I write this letter with no expectations whatsoever. I write it to put painful memories behind me.

I thought, until yesterday, that I had forgiven you for what I felt was a betrayal of friendship, trust, and mutual respect. Today I feel I just shoved it on the back burner and every time any resentment comes up now, I push it further back. This does not engender peace.

I say again, I expect nothing from you. It's not about money. It never was. To me it's about friendship, and all that goes with it. I was disappointed.

The letting go of my resentment is the most important thing for me to do right now. It's important because resentment is a weight I no longer wish to carry.

So I do forgive you. I forgive you with the hope that this will free any negative energy that we may harbor between us.

I wish you well.

Everything is forgivable, and when we truly realize that nursing a grievance is injurious to our health and happiness, we can let go. Forgiveness doesn't mean that we condone or agree with what happened; it simply means that we're willing to heal our own minds by no longer seeing any value in holding on to anger.

The Forgiveness Teacher

— Jerry and Diane

A few years ago, we traveled to Ghana, West Africa, to experience and learn from the work being done there in Attitudinal Healing. Mary Clottey—the executive director of the Center for Attitudinal Healing in the capital, Accra—shared the following story.

Mary taught in a grammar school where there was a lot of fighting among the students. Using the Principles of Attitudinal Healing, she helped the children learn ways of communicating with each other without anger or violence. In fact, her kids often referred to her as "the forgiveness teacher."

One ten-year-old boy had been a real terror who fought with everyone and disrupted everything around him. Wherever he went, he seemed to break things, although he never accepted any responsibility for his actions. One day he was caught stealing money from his teacher's purse. The principal jumped in and called for an assembly of the entire school. According to the tradition of that school, the boy was to be whipped with a cane up on the stage while the students and faculty were forced to watch. The principal wanted to make an example of this boy and then expel him.

On the appointed day, the entire school assembled in the auditorium where the punishment was to be carried out. As the boy was led onto the stage, Mary, who had previously tried to prevent the caning, began to slowly stand up. Just as she was about to call out, "Forgive him," all the little children around her leapt to their feet.

"Forgive him, forgive him, forgive him," the children around her began to chant. Soon, more students from other grades joined in on the chorus: "Forgive him, forgive him, forgive him." Finally, all the kids in the assembly rose as one and chanted over and over, "Forgive him."

Obviously stunned by this, the principal and the boy stared out into the audience, and then the child broke down and began to sob. The principal embraced the boy, and immediately the atmosphere of the assembly had changed from one of anger and fear to one of compassion and love . . . all because a teacher had the courage to stand up.

The boy was neither caned nor expelled. Instead, he was forgiven and loved—not by just the students, but by the principal and teachers as well. From that day forward, he didn't get into a single fight, break or steal anything, or act at all disruptively. As the year progressed, he even became an excellent student and also made lots of new friends.

Many people at the school believed that the principal's action of calling the assembly to punish this boy was too harsh. But the principal was also forgiven, and in the process the seeds for a new, more loving environment were sowed.

When we hold on to grievances, we bring darkness
into our minds and into the world. When we forgive
and love, the Light shines the darkness away. Love
is the most powerful healing force in the world.

Finding Compassion Where There Is None

— Diane

Recently, two friends came to dinner in Hawaii and during the course of the evening, shared their anger and anguish over the treatment a neighbor was receiving from her son. Since they considered themselves a compassionate and spiritually aware couple, they were even more disturbed by their inability to release their anger and judgments about the son.

The neighbor had been suffering with a long illness, and our friends were part of her volunteer caregiving team. The son lived on the mainland, and he wasn't just distant from his mother in miles, but personally and financially as well. He showed virtually no interest in her well-being or the state of care she was receiving. However, now that she was near death, he'd come to Hawaii to get her to fund a business venture he was trying to launch. This lack of concern for his dying mother made our friends furious.

After talking with them for a long while, it was clear that nothing we said would budge them from their judgments about this man, despite the fact that they wanted to see the situation differently and desired some way to bring a sense of compassion into their minds.

While the wife and I were in the kitchen, I felt her distress even more clearly. As I pulled the dinner from the oven, I silently asked for guidance to help these two beautiful people. Casserole in hand, I turned from the oven and what came out of my mouth was: "I feel compassion for this man because at the very least, he still has to live out the rest of his life as himself. He has to take all that he thinks, says, and does with him the entire journey. That's a lot to live with."

A lightbulb went on within her that literally illuminated her face. She went to her husband and shared my comment, and he too immediately brightened. They both expressed to me that this was the shift in their belief system that allowed them to forgive the son, and they later wrote to say that it had a lasting effect.

When we're stuck in our judgments about someone,
it can be helpful to get a change of perspective by
feeling the burden of the other person's thinking.

The House of Guilt

— Jerry

Guilt was the foundation of my family life. It was the bread and butter of my meals, the very air I breathed. So pervasive was it that at times I wondered if there was a guilt gene, and we had all inherited it! Guilt was also my parents' favorite control tool: "Finish your plate—there are children starving in India," "Don't eat bacon or God will strike you dead." These are just samples of warnings I received on a daily basis.

Consequently, decision making was extremely difficult because I was terrified of making a mistake—which, of course, led to the very thing I feared. As a child, I was hyperactive, clumsy, always spilling things, and generally just made a mess wherever I went. Everything I did seemed wrong. If my parents had frowns on their faces, I always assumed that I was to blame. Wherever I went, a cloud of guilt hovered over me.

My guilt prevented me from taking up a spiritual path, because I thought that God was just waiting for me to make a mistake so that "He" could punish me. It is impossible to love and trust what we fear. Diane and I now understand that the ego's law of guilt causes us either to punish and attack ourselves or to project our guilt onto others so that we can attack *them.*

We have learned that our guilt blocks peace, imprisoning our minds, and shackles us to an endless cycle of condemnation and depression. It separates us from our Source and from our brothers and sisters because we remain stuck in our own misery. It is an emotional place to hide that has little to do with genuine values or conscience. In fact, the guilt we choose to hold on to is often a psychological tool with which we try to control other people or ourselves. It is impossible to experience both guilt and love at the same time.

*Only by recognizing that holding on to guilt has no
value can we turn from it toward the peace that is
ours when we take responsibility and practice love and
forgiveness. We can choose to say good-bye to guilt.*

Forgiving an Ex

— Jerry

In 1973 after 20 years of marriage, my wife, Pat, and I went through a painful and angry divorce. It was so bad that I'd given up all hope that we would ever forgive each other or ourselves. I certainly never thought we could be friends again.

When I consciously began a spiritual journey, forgiveness was the central part of it, and we both made a great effort to let go of the painful past. Pat later remarried, and she, her new husband, and her father came to Seattle to hear me lecture. Since she was living near Tacoma, I had breakfast with the three of them the following day. Pat told me that she liked everything I'd said. I thought that a miracle must be occurring because she'd liked almost nothing I said when we were married!

After returning home to Tiburon, California, I was very proud of myself and told everyone I knew that this forgiveness stuff really works. A few months later my son Lee informed me that he had just learned that his mom and new stepfather were moving to Tiburon. My immediate thought was: *Oh no! We'll be shopping at the same market and going to the same restaurants. This can't be happening!* Clearly, I had more forgiveness work to do—I hadn't released the past completely. I obviously had been given more homework, so I got right on it.

Pat's marriage didn't last, and within a few years she married for a third time. Knowing I was a pretty good photographer, she invited me to take pictures at the wedding. Some of the guests considered it a bit unusual for the ex-husband to also be the photographer! Pat, Diane, and I continued to be the best of friends. We shared family events and holidays together for over two decades, and Diane and I became a strong part of Pat's support during her years of declining health.

After a long illness, Pat died in 2007. At the beautiful memorial service atop the hills of Marin, a family friend shared how inspiring our joined family had been to so many others. She also shared that Pat's obituary was probably the only one on record that stated she was survived by her beloved ex-husband, Jerry Jampolsky, and his wife, Diane Cirincione. We truly do believe that there is enough love to go around for everyone and that no one need be left out of love.

*Before we can hope to have a healthy, happy
relationship with our current partner, it's essential
to completely forgive our ex. Otherwise we carry anger
and judgment into our new relationship, which will be
polluted. It's important to remember that forgiveness
is a gift we give ourselves as well as those we love.*

Gratitude

— *Diane*

Win Vu's journey has been an odyssey few of us could imagine, and his inner strength and courage continue to inspire us. The oldest of three, he was just a child when his father was imprisoned for six years in Vietnam at the height of the war. Along with his mother, he became the forager for food and protector for his fragmented family, who barely survived starvation during his father's incarceration.

When he was about eight, the family attempted to escape Vietnam but failed. The following year, they risked imprisonment and death to try again with their father. This time they succeeded in leaving their homeland, only to embark on a nightmarish journey as refugees for the next year. They were called "the boat people," a group of desperately courageous families who sailed away from persecution in small fishing boats toward the United States in search of freedom and a better way of life. When Win Vu wasn't yet ten, they settled in Atlanta, Georgia, where they began their new lives.

Win Vu became part of the Children as Teachers of Peace (CATOP) project that Jerry founded in 1981 and launched with Jehan Sadat, widow of assassinated president Anwar Sadat of Egypt. CATOP encouraged young people between 7 and 17 to travel to foreign lands. The destinations were always places that were engaged in conflicts with the U.S., such as China, Russia, and Nicaragua. In a totally nonpolitical way, the children were given the opportunity to "see the faces of the enemy and decide for themselves." Many countries participated over the course of the next ten years, and some even beyond that.

Win Vu was about 15 when he joined us in the first group of American children to visit the People's Republic of China in 70 years. This courageous young man faced and overcame his fear of the Chinese and proved to be an immeasurable asset to the group. He has grown to be an extraordinary adult, dedicated to supporting peace and serving the needs of his fellow human beings. Throughout the years, we've remained close to him and have been able to accompany him on his journey of maturation and growth.

On one occasion, we invited Win Vu to join us when we were asked to speak to a large gathering of inner-city high school students in a tough area of Atlanta. Most of them were African Americans, and from their body language, it was clear that the big guys in the audience were extremely skeptical that this skinny little Asian guy who looked about eight could tell them anything.

Standing silently alone up on the huge convention stage, he looked fragile and hesitant as he scanned the restless and reluctant audience. In his quiet, gentle way, he then told them the story of his young life in Vietnam and what he and his family had to overcome to make it to Atlanta. He soon had the absolute attention of every kid in the room. They sat at the edge of their seats as he softly and simply stated the reality: that he and his family narrowly escaped death just about every day of their lives before entering the United States. Even afterward, language and culture barriers were daily hurdles they would face for years to come.

Win Vu then said something that very likely moved everyone within earshot—something *we* remember to this day, nearly 20 years later. He walked closer to the edge of the stage, looked right at the audience, and with deep sincerity said, "I know that your lives are hard and that you may often think that you're at the bottom of the social and economic ladder here in America, looking up at everyone else. But what you probably don't realize is that the rest of the world is actually looking up at *you*. Even though you don't have as much as other Americans, you have so very much more than everybody else on the planet. Be grateful for that, and think about what your life *is* and not what it is *not*."

This final comment completely silenced the room as they sat motionless, staring at him. Suddenly, they began applauding and then stood as one to give him a resounding ovation.

After the lecture, a group of large, tough-looking teens came up and took the young speaker off to "hang with them" and to attend their classes for the day. The principal later told us that Win Vu had a life-changing impact on the students. Today Win Vu is a pediatric cardiologist, helping to heal the hearts of children.

No matter how difficult or deprived our lives have been,
it's always possible for us to turn from anger, judgment,
and blame. Doing so affirms our faith in ourselves and is
the first step toward a new life. An attitude of deprivation
begets misery; an attitude of thanks creates <u>miracles.</u>

$\mathscr{T}$rees and Open Hands

— Jerry

Following my divorce, I felt shattered, depressed, and fragmented. I needed a new focus, something that would take my mind off my pain. I took a course in photography at College of Marin north of San Francisco, and for a year afterward, I'd drive deep into Marin County to photograph oak trees and redwoods. I framed the prints and hung them throughout my "bachelor" pad.

Although I wasn't consciously aware of it at the time, I think that I concentrated on these enormous trees because of their deep roots and the fact that their branches reached toward the sun and the sky. Symbolically, this helped me reestablish my own roots. The ancient redwoods of Muir Woods seemed sacred and gave me a sense of peace at a time when my life seemed chaotic and lonely. Photographing these thousand-year-old survivors from the once-lush forests of Northern California was profoundly healing, but the feeling of harmony I experienced there would never continue once I returned home.

In 1975, after I consciously began my spiritual path, I became aware of many things I was attached to and how I was making my peace of mind dependent on external objects and events. I recognized that if I truly wanted to receive guidance from a Higher Power, I needed to let go of these attachments; and although I worked hard, I was having trouble doing so.

144

One day I had the idea of taking photographs of people's empty hands, which I framed and put on the walls of my apartment. These served to remind me to come to God with empty hands. I discovered that when I released my ego needs and desires, I reached a deeper level of peace that endured.

Our egos want to control every situation—this is a given.
If we hope to access inner guidance, it's most helpful
to come with empty hands, holding on to nothing.

Friendship

— Jerry

From the very beginning and on the deepest level possible, Diane and I have always felt a profound and tender soul connection. When we met, there was a bright, gentle light in her eyes, which went through me, from the top of my head to the tips of my toes.

But there were many things on the surface that caused both of us conflicts. Once again my old feelings about how unsafe it is to trust emerged, and they mingled with my unresolved issues of jealousy and possessiveness, which I mistakenly believed I'd gotten past. Old films of mine began to run again. I learned that I'd buried a lot of issues about personal relationships rather than trying to work them out. We both had guilt from the past, and there were many times when we had thoughts of going in opposite directions—of running away from each other.

One evening about three years into our relationship, I found myself becoming furious with Diane because she wasn't fitting into the mold my mind had made for her. That can be translated into: *Diane wasn't doing what I wanted her to do.*

She'd often and deliberately spoken to me about wanting to go to Lake Tahoe to learn to ski better and had explained how relevant, on many levels, this was to her personal growth. Because she'd so frequently set this desire aside to please someone else, she now wanted to change that pattern. Not being a skier myself, and fueled by my own insecurities and jealousy about her going without me, I downplayed the importance of her need.

A few weeks prior to her planned ski trip, my own trip to the Sudan came up. Diane had previously and clearly told me that she felt that my itinerary was potentially too exhausting for me both physically and emotionally. I thanked her for her concern and chose not to alter my plans.

Just before I left for North Africa, she said, "Jerry, I go on record that this trip is potentially too taxing for you and not a good idea as planned. That being said, I wish you well. Please remember that just two days after you return, I leave for my four-day ski trip to Lake Tahoe, the one I've been planning all year. You need to know that I'm definitely going, regardless of what happens on *your* trip." I agreed, and off I went to the Sudan.

The devastation, starvation, and death from the drought in this desert region were beyond anything I'd ever encountered. It was a life-changing event, but I did my work there and got on the plane to return home to California. My guilt about leaving people starving on the ground and then being given a full meal on the flight was so great that my back went out. When we landed, I disembarked from the plane debilitated and in serious pain. When I got home, I could barely function or even walk around.

Diane came over and lovingly took care of me. I assumed that two days later she wouldn't go skiing, fulfilling my secret wish that she not go. As the day ended and she turned to leave, she announced that she'd see me in four days and would call from the mountains. Indignant, I said that I couldn't believe she was going skiing and was just leaving me there somewhat incapacitated.

As she was putting her coat on, she turned to me and simply asked, "Jerry, are you going to die?"

Stunned by the question, I replied, "No, of course not."

She said, "Then I'm going skiing"—and off she went.

I began to interpret Diane's very healthy independence as a sign that she was rejecting me, and I ignored all the spiritual principles I'd been trying to apply to my life. In the heat of my anger, which I considered righteous and justified, I did everything I could think of to make her wrong and me right. Once again I'd chosen to be right instead of happy.

I went to bed that night feeling enraged, bitter, and depressed. However, as my head hit the pillow, I had enough sanity left to ask God for help. I wanted peace of mind, not the inner agitation I was feeling. At about 2 A.M., I awoke with a deep urge to write. What came out was a meditation on my friendship with Diane that I and many others have found helpful. It's now printed on a poster that also has a photograph of my parents holding hands when they were 90 years old. This writing has helped me look at friendship in an entirely different way.

Friendship

I thank you for teaching me:

. . . what friendship is—a relationship that has no needs, where one's interest in the other person's welfare is the same as one's interest in oneself.

. . . that friendship is a state of mind where there is no fear, no guilt, no attack thoughts, no feelings of vulnerability; where it is all right for you and others to see me as I really am; where there is constant giving and forgiving; where the only desire is to be helpful, gentle, and patient; where there is no past or future, but only the present; where each instant is for total loving and letting go; and where there is no holding on, no attachments, and no demands.

. . . that friendship is a relationship where there is only light, only the joining and sharing of love, and there is no exclusiveness; where the geographical location and physical separation is of absolutely no importance; and where there is complete and total love and acceptance regardless of the illusory perceptions of separation made by time and space.

. . . that friendship is eternal—a state where no thoughts, words, or deeds can cause any feeling of hurt or separation and where the light of Spirit is the only reality.

. . . that true friendship is a state of bliss, where we see only the God Self in each other. It is a state of inner knowing that we are connected by love, with each other and God, forever.

Once again I discovered that learning could come out of personal conflict, and that I could choose to change my perceptions of a relationship, myself, and the world. How grateful I was to realize that the time it takes to change my mind and to experience peace was totally up to me. With a shift in my perception, the basis for a whole new connection with Diane began.

It became very clear to Diane and me that our relationship wouldn't work unless both of us committed ourselves to putting our spiritual journey first in our lives. We began doing our best to free ourselves of all attachments and to "love and let go" each day. Prayer and meditation became daily essentials.

Each day, we make a sincere effort to let go of our own plans and allow Spirit to lead the way. There are still plenty of occasions when we get caught in the busy-ness of the day and forget to be still and to step aside, but we're learning that when this happens, we can take time to decide once again: *Do we want peace or conflict? Are we choosing love or fear?*

With my past relationships, I always had a plan for the form they were to take and felt that I needed assurance that this form would stay the same. So it became quite a new experience for me not to prescribe how things would evolve.

As we've worked together for close to three decades, doing our best to listen to our own individual guidance, we've noticed a greater balance between the male and female aspects in each of us. If there's one key to the success we've had in helping ourselves and others, it's that we make every effort to feel our own wholeness in relationship with our Creator.

There's a very significant prayer adapted from the *Course* that we say before every meeting, lecture, or workshop we conduct. It's a quick way to lay aside our egos, let go of fear, and allow the light to shine in us, helping us know what we should think, say, and do. It goes like this:

I am here only to be truly helpful.
I am here to represent You Who sent me.
I do not have to worry about what to say or what to do,
because You Who sent me will direct me.
I am content to be wherever You wish,
knowing You go there with me.
I will be healed as I let You teach me to heal.

$\mathcal{T}$rusting Guidance

— Jerry

In 1980 I was preparing to go to Israel to lecture at a number of hospitals. Since I'd never been there before, I was also looking forward to visiting various historical sites.

I'd already made my airline reservations, but two weeks before I was to leave, I received guidance that I was to go to Egypt immediately after my lectures. My reaction was that this notion was crazy and I should ignore it . . . but each day, my inner message grew stronger. I finally decided to purchase a ticket to Egypt, but my ego still insisted that doing so was insane: Not only would I miss seeing the sights in Israel, but I didn't even know anyone in Cairo. I told a friend that the only reason I could think of for going was that I might meet Madame Jehan Sadat—the wife of Egypt's president and a woman who was actively improving the health, welfare, and civil rights of her people. I also hoped to visit the new hospital that she'd been instrumental in founding.

In those days, you couldn't fly directly from Israel to Egypt, so I traveled to Greece, then on to Cairo. On the flight, I read the airline magazine, which had an article about a Dr. Shabander who was a cancer specialist in Cairo. I arrived there Thursday night and went directly to my hotel. I still had no idea what I was doing and began to wonder why I'd listened to that inner voice.

The following morning, I asked the front-desk clerk if he could give me the phone number of Dr. Shabander. I finally reached the man and asked if it would be possible for us to get together that day. He informed me that Fridays in Egypt were nonbusiness days, like Sundays in the United States, and that he was just leaving and couldn't meet with me.

I thanked him anyway; then there was a pause, and he said he could see me for a few minutes if I took a cab to his home, which I did. He was a wonderful man, and we immediately had a feeling of closeness. He invited me to join him and his wife at a party they were attending that evening.

When we arrived, I discovered that President Sadat's cabinet was also attending. I spent a fair amount of time with the minister of health, who invited me to his office the following Monday. After talking to me for an hour, he excused himself for a moment. When he returned, he told me that he'd arranged a 20-minute interview with Madame Sadat on Monday afternoon. I remembered the off-the-cuff remark I'd made about possibly meeting her and got goose bumps. My 20-minute interview turned into two hours, and she invited me to visit the hospital the next day.

When I returned to California, I knew that I'd learned a valuable lesson about respecting my inner guidance. My rational mind had insisted that I was acting in an illogical—even crazy—way, but I had still trusted the voice inside. This was a big step forward for me, although I was still somewhat leery.

A year later I was helping to organize a large conference in San Jose, California, for our Children as Teachers of Peace project. While meditating one day, I received guidance to invite Madame Sadat, but my inner dialogue went like this: *Madame Sadat sees hundreds of people. She won't even remember who I am, so it would be a waste of time to invite her.* But the guidance persisted, so finally I sent her a brief invitation. Four weeks later, when I was lecturing in New York City, I received a call from my secretary, who told me that Madame Sadat's secretary was trying to reach me.

She accepted my invitation, and this would be the first time she'd left Egypt following her husband's assassination in 1981.

While in California, she visited our Center, and she and I later lectured together in the Netherlands and England. We developed a close relationship, and she invited Diane and me to visit her in Egypt and give a few lectures there.

Learning to trust our inner guidance isn't easy, but it's important if we're to have faith in our spiritual path. The ego mind is small, separate, and often afraid; and its counsel represents this. The voice of love is without limitation, and there's no fear within its guidance.

Pleasing vs. Loving

— Jerry

For much of my life, I struggled unsuccessfully to get my mother's approval. My futile attempts could fill several books by themselves, but as someone who believes in forgiveness and unconditional love, I have to thank my mom for having provided me with so many opportunities to practice what I believe!

When I was 58, my mother needed a new physician. I knew that she neither liked nor respected young doctors, whom she considered inexperienced and "wet behind the ears." Knowing this, I naïvely thought to please her by choosing an older one who was my age. When I told her about the new physician, she asked exactly what I knew she would: "How old is he?"

I confidently replied, "Mom, he's an older, seasoned doctor who's my age."

With equal certainty, she said, "I don't want a young doctor your age who doesn't know what he's doing. You go out and get me an older one."

Another time when I visited her in a retirement community, I checked her mailbox before going to see her, but it was empty. When I got to her room, the first thing she asked me was whether I'd picked up her mail. I told her that I'd checked, but she hadn't received any. She started screaming at me, calling me a liar and accusing me of not wanting to stop by her mailbox. The only thing that calmed her down was my willingness to go back and check it again.

While lecturing in British Columbia, I called my mom to check in and see how she was doing. She asked me where I was, and I told her. Her reply was: "You're lying. I don't believe you're in British Columbia. I think you're still in San Francisco and just don't want to visit your lonely mother."

Then she surprised me by saying, "Give me the phone number where you are. I'm going to *prove* that you're not in Canada but still in San Francisco." I gave her the number, and the phone rang a few minutes later. Since she'd placed the call through an operator, I knew that she could hear me, but she told the operator she couldn't, and hung up.

A week later when I visited her, I asked why she'd said she couldn't hear me. Her reply was: "I'm not going to pay my good money just to hear your voice long-distance!" Then she changed the subject.

*If we're going to heal our relationship with
our parents and family members, it's essential to
recognize that they don't have to change. At times
it may help to be open to doing something that can
seem illogical to us if it brings them comfort. And
it definitely helps to have a healthy sense of humor!*

*Unconditional love is just that: It isn't dependent
on the actions of others. There are some people
we'll never please, yet we can still love them.*

Meeting Challenges
with Love

— Jerry and Diane

Several years ago we met Michael Kanouff in Maui, Hawaii. Some years before, he'd been playing Frisbee on the beach and when he lunged for the disk, he tripped, fell on his head, and severed his spinal cord. He's now a quadriplegic.

Like many quadriplegics, he's had challenges, one of the most bothersome being a series of bladder infections that have been painful and difficult to treat. As a professional photographer, he'd been self-sufficient and extremely active. Suddenly he found himself not only unable to walk, but also dependent on other people. It takes him about three hours to get ready in the morning and another three to prepare for bed at the end of the day.

Through all of this, Michael has retained his sense of humor and his zest for life. He also has a Website where he helps others with similar problems. He's an inspiration because of his courage and "never give up" attitude.

A few years ago, along with fellow authors Wayne Dyer and Alan Cohen, we participated in a fund-raising event for Michael. The money that was generated allowed him to go to Miami for a spinal-cord evaluation and also helped provide him with a special van.

Two years ago, a beautiful angel entered his life in the form of Kimberly. Her inner and outer beauty is immediately apparent—she's a light for all who meet her. She began as one of Michael's many caregivers, and they later married. It would be difficult to find a couple who exudes more love for each other. It's a blessing to be in their presence. Gradually Kimberly has taken over almost all of Michael's care, so they no longer have to cope with people who may or may not be dependable.

One night when we were having dinner with them, we asked Kimberly, "If you were to give advice to a newly wedded spouse of a quadriplegic, what would you say?"

She replied, "I'd remind them that love is what their life is all about. I don't think of the things I do for Michael as work. For me, they're acts of love that give me great pleasure. It all has to do with your attitude." In turn, Michael spends a great deal of his time helping other people with physical challenges via the Internet.

We all know that life is full of tragedy and challenges.
Often we have little or no control over what happens to our
bodies, but what we can control are our attitudes. No matter
what happens to us or to someone we love, we can choose
to react with acceptance, peace, and a spirit of generosity.

Practicing What We Believe

— Jerry and Diane

We met Franklin Levinson in Maui, where he'd moved to explore his passion for horses after a successful singing career in Florida. He started a business called Adventures On Horseback and took people for rides in "old Hawaii." Our children and grandkids bonded with him and remain his good friends.

Franklin incorporated Attitudinal Healing into his life and his work with horses. He has written several articles, one of which is titled "Attitude is Everything with Horses and Humans." He's told us many stories, but the one that stands out is about a teenage girl with cancer.

When she arrived for her ride, Franklin wasn't prepared for what he saw: She had only one arm, her other one having been amputated due to her disease. Since she was quite frail, Franklin worried that she might lose her balance, fall, and badly injure herself. This "fear thinking" progressed to the possibility of his being sued. He recognized that he had to stop the anxiety, so he went behind a tree to still his mind and ask for guidance—which told him to allow her to ride.

She had an amazing experience and not only held her balance but was quite proficient. About six months later she died. Her father traveled to Hawaii to thank Franklin because his daughter had written about her ride in a diary, describing the day as one of the most important and beautiful experiences of her life. She wrote that the love and compassion Franklin extended her empowered her to have more confidence in herself.

Franklin now lives near Aspen, Colorado, where he conducts "horse whispering" classes. He works with a variety of people from all walks of life, including physically challenged children and adults. His Website is **www.wayofthehorse.org**.

There's no place we can't practice simple kindness, patience, love, and integrity—which are the essence of true spirituality. And it's our willingness to adopt these attitudes that also affirms our faith and leaves no area of life outside our devotion.

The Lemon Tree

— Diane

When my mom and stepdad, Larry, moved into their retirement condominium in Northern California a few years back, one planter remained from the previous owners. It was cobalt blue and sat about 30 inches high on the right side of their beautiful lanai. While the pot was lovely, at its center—in the middle of the soil—a five-inch-high dead stick awkwardly protruded.

After I mentioned to Larry how beautiful a bed of mixed flowers would look in the planter, he paused a moment, then said, "No, I want to keep it the way it is."

"But Pop," I pleaded, "this thing is dead. Why not let me just pull it out?" The discussion went back and forth until I finally understood that he really wanted it there. Alas, the ugly stick remained.

Larry adopted this stick. He watered, nourished, and protected it with all his tender loving care. Maybe the fragile, declining state of his own body sensitized him to the plight of this dead-looking plant, but in some way he bonded with it and made its safety and well-being his own responsibility.

Weeks passed, and then one day a bud appeared . . . which grew into a branch . . . which sprouted a leaf. More buds appeared, and Larry realized that his precious plant was a lemon tree. Spring came and went, and as his health declined, the tree continued to grow. He taught Jorge, his caregiver and dear friend, how to continue to tend to the tree after he was gone, which Jorge did with great love and attention.

Early one morning in late July, Larry died peacefully. After that, the lemon tree began to flourish, with branches and leaves bursting out all over. It extended its reach and expanded many feet wide and high, but there were no signs of any lemons.

Around the second anniversary of Larry's death, lemons appeared and grew to perfection—I've never seen such a healthy lemon tree. While visiting Mom, I noticed bowls of the fruit in the kitchen and discovered that they'd all come from Pop's tree. She was so pleased, and offering me some to take home, she said, "There were 35 lemons on Larry's tree. Isn't that amazing?" I agreed that it was.

Just then, something happened that literally stopped me in my tracks. In my head I heard what sounded like Larry's voice say *36,* so I suggested, "Mom, maybe you had 36 lemons, instead of 35."

She looked at me oddly and said quite clearly, "No, I'm sure I had 35 because I specifically counted them."

As I started to answer "Okay" and drop the subject, I once again heard the voice declare, with a bit more emphasis, *There were 36.* A bit confounded, I turned directly to her and said, "Mom, I'm getting that there were 36 lemons, not 35."

She adamantly maintained that she was positive there were 35. Having no idea what this all meant and ready to let it drop, I turned to go back inside the house. Just as I did, I heard the much firmer, internally audible voice of Larry say, *Tell her there were 36 lemons, one for each year.* I spun around and bent over my mom, who was sitting on the lanai. I looked into her eyes and in a serious, confident voice stated, "Mom, Larry just told me to tell you that there were 36 lemons, one for each year you were married."

She looked distressed as she said, "But there were only 35."

I insisted, "Mom, there must be another lemon somewhere because I know in my gut that what I heard is true."

She sat there looking puzzled and thinking hard. I left the lanai and went to the kitchen. A few minutes later, she excitedly called out to me, "Diane, Diane, there *were* 36 lemons! Just the other day Sister Kathryn stayed over, and she told me she picked one of Pop's lemons to use for our breakfast. This was before I removed the others and counted them. There were 36 lemons!" With tears of joy in our eyes and smiles on our lips, we embraced for a long time.

The lemon tree has flourished by our home each and every year, continuing to remind us that where there is love, nothing is impossible.

Because our minds are joined, we don't need bodies
to communicate with those we love. Within oneness
there's no separation; there's only eternal love.

$\mathscr{A}$fterword

What have we learned on our journey? Perhaps one of the most important lessons is that it's our egos that make life seem so complicated and complex. Happily, our lives can also be greatly simplified and balanced when we consciously direct our thoughts, words, and actions toward love rather than fear.

We lose our way home when we're following the signposts of . . .

- . . . grudges and grievances.

- . . . judgments and unforgiveness.

- . . . anger and hatred.

- . . . greed and prejudice.

- . . . victimhood and self-pity.

- . . . lack of honesty and integrity.

- . . . projections and misperceptions.

- . . . condemnations of self and/or others.

- . . . lack of kindness, empathy, and compassion.

We've found that we know we're on the right road when . . .

- . . . peace of mind becomes our single goal.

- . . . love and forgiveness are as important as breathing.

- . . . we're focused on joining rather than separation.

- . . . caring for another is the same as caring for ourselves.

- . . . cooperation means more than competition.

- . . . giving is a higher priority than getting.

- . . . we choose to let go of all our judgments and grievances.

We experience our connection with everyone and everything when . . .

- . . . we practice love and forgiveness with each step of our journey.

- . . . we see others as our sisters and brothers.

- . . . compassion, kindness, generosity, tenderness, and gentleness are in our every heartbeat.

We've found that it's helpful to remind ourselves throughout the day . . .

- . . . to value a still mind rather than a busy mind.

- . . . to be a vessel of love and compassion regardless of others' behavior.

- . . . to treat our relationship with everyone we meet or think about as sacred and holy.

- . . . to find new ways each day of sharing how much we love and treasure all human beings.

- . . . to resist the temptation to make our to-do list our "god."

- . . . to look upon every experience as a positive lesson we can learn from.

- . . . to laugh more, to leave "miles of smiles," and not to take ourselves so seriously.

May the compass of our life
and the rudder of our ship
be love and forgiveness.

May our gratitude be expressed
as we walk in love.
May all our thoughts,
words, and actions
express honesty and integrity.
And may the place
of everlasting love
be our true Home now
and forevermore.

Appendix

What Is Attitudinal Healing?

Attitudinal Healing is based on the belief that neither individuals nor external situations cause us to be upset. Rather, conflict and distress are the result of our thoughts, feelings, and attitudes about people and events. Attitudinal Healing allows us to let go of fear and negative, hurtful thoughts from the past; correct our misperceptions; and remove the inner obstacles to peace.

It begins with the willingness to find another way of looking at the world, at life, and at death, making peace of mind our only goal and forgiveness our primary function. It's about discovering the negative effect that holding on to grievances, blaming others, and condemning ourselves has so that we can choose to no longer find value in them.

Attitudinal Healing asserts that when we let go of fear, only love remains—and this is the answer to every problem we face in life. It's the recognition that our true reality never changes, and that love is all there is.

Attitudinal Healing views the purpose of all communication as joining and regards happiness as a choice. It recognizes that we're all worthy of love and that happiness is our own responsibility as well as our natural state of being.

Attitudinal Healing acknowledges that our only function is forgiveness. Rather than making decisions based on a fearful past, we can learn to make them by listening to the inner voice of love.

The Principles of Attitudinal Healing

1. The essence of our being is love.

2. Health is inner peace. Healing is letting go of fear.

3. Giving and receiving are the same.

4. We can let go of the past and the future.

5. Now is the only time there is, and each instant is for giving.

6. We can learn to love ourselves and others by forgiving rather than judging.

7. We can become love finders rather than faultfinders.

8. We can choose to direct ourselves to be peaceful inside regardless of what is happening outside.

9. We are students and teachers to each other.

10. We can focus on the whole of life rather than the fragments.

11. Since love is eternal, death need not be viewed as fearful.

12. We can always perceive ourselves and others as either extending love or giving a call for help.

The International Center for Attitudinal Healing (ICAH) is a nonprofit community-health organization founded in 1975 in Marin County, California, by Dr. Jerry Jampolsky and friends in order to provide emotional healing for children, adolescents, and adults of all ages dealing with the multiple challenges of daily stress, a life crisis, or chronic or life-threatening illness.

Dr. Jampolsky created the "peer support group" model that recognizes that peace of mind and relief from a personal life crisis are best achieved when individuals help others. All of the support services at the Center remain free of charge and rely primarily on donations and volunteers. ICAH is now in 28 countries, helping individuals cope with chronic or life-threatening illness such as metastases and HIV/AIDS, loss and grief, and the trauma of war. In addition, it offers training to government agencies, prison programs, and "The Power to Choose" school project, educating teachers and grades K–12 in concepts in Attitudinal Healing.

For more than 30 years, the Center has responded to the needs of the community, and through the continued generosity and support of individuals, it will make these much-needed services available for generations to come.

For more information about the International Center for Attitudinal Healing in Sausalito, California; its workshops; or other Centers around the world, please go to: **www.attitudinalhealing.org**, call **(415) 331-6161**, or fax **(415) 331-4545**.

Acknowledgments

Deep gratitude goes to our longtime friend Gayle Prather for her gift of editing. We want to also acknowledge all the people who inspired the stories compiled here, as well as those who have traveled the journey with us from the International Centers for Attitudinal Healing around the world, and who have been such powerful teachers and way-showers on the journey to find our way Home.

About the Authors

Gerald Jampolsky, M.D., is a graduate of Stanford University School of Medicine and is a child and adult psychiatrist. He founded the first International Center for Attitudinal Healing in 1975. There are now Centers and groups located on five continents offering free psychological, emotional, and spiritual support for children and adults facing crisis/growth situations—including life-threatening illnesses, caregiver issues, and relationship challenges—as well as a host of other services.

Diane V. Cirincione, Ph.D., is a therapist, businesswoman, international lecturer, and author/co-author of several books. In addition to holding master's and Ph.D. degrees in Clinical Psychology, she also has a B.S. in Organizational Behavior. She has founded and owned four companies and has worked with Jerry since 1981, responding to requests from around the world to adapt Attitudinal Healing to diverse, culturally appropriate situations.

Jerry and Diane are married and reside in Hawaii and Northern California. They are both on the Advisory Board of the International Center for Attitudinal Healing as well as serving on the faculty of the University of Hawaii's John A. Burns School of Medicine, Department of Complementary and Alternative Medicine.

Singly or together they have written *Love Is Letting Go of Fear; Change Your Mind, Change Your Life; Forgiveness: The Greatest Healer of All; Love Is the Answer; A Mini Course for Life;* and a dozen other books, published in more than 30 languages.

Over the last 25 years, they have been invited to work cross-culturally in 54 countries and have both been the recipients of numerous international humanitarian awards. In 2005, Jerry received one of the American Medical Association's highest honors, the *Excellence in Medicine–Pride in the Profession Award,* for his contribution of Attitudinal Healing to the mental-health field, for his inspiration to others, and for his decades of humanitarian service.

To learn more about the books, lectures, seminars, and outreach work of Jerry Jampolsky and Diane Cirincione, please go to: **www.JerryJampolsky.com** or **www.DianeCirincione.com.** For their audios, videos, CDs, and DVDs, go to: **www.zipidee.com/ jerryanddiane**.

For information about the International Center for Attitudinal Healing in Sausalito, California; its workshops; or other Centers around the world, please visit: **www.attitudinalhealing.org**, or contact:

The International Center for Attitudinal Healing
33 Buchanan Drive
Sausalito, CA 94965
Phone: (415) 331-6161
Fax: (415) 331-4545

Hay House Titles of Related Interest

YOU CAN HEAL YOUR LIFE, the movie,
starring Louise L. Hay & Friends
(available as a 1-DVD program and an expanded 2-DVD set)
Watch the trailer at: **www.LouiseHayMovie.com**

Inspiration: Your Ultimate Calling, by Dr. Wayne W. Dyer

*DailyOM: Inspirational Thoughts for a Happy, Healthy,
and Fulfilling Day,* by Madisyn Taylor

The Guru of Joy: Sri Sri Ravi Shankar & the Art of Living,
by François Gautier

*If I Can Forgive, So Can You: My Autobiography of How
I Overcame My Past and Healed My Life,* by Denise Linn

The Last Dropout: Stop the Epidemic! by Bill Milliken

Led by Faith: Learning to Trust God in All Things,
by Immaculée Ilibagiza, with Steve Erwin
(available September 2008)

*The Times of Our Lives: Extraordinary True Stories of Synchronicity,
Destiny, Meaning, and Purpose,* by Louise L. Hay & Friends

Wisdom of the Heart: Inspiration for a Life Worth Living,
by Alan Cohen

Your Soul's Compass: What Is Spiritual Guidance?
by Joan Z. Borysenko, Ph.D., and Gordon Franklin Dveirin, Ed.D.

All of the above are available at your local bookstore,
or may be ordered by contacting Hay House (see next page).

We hope you enjoyed this Hay House book. If you'd like to receive a free catalog featuring additional Hay House books and products, or if you'd like information about the Hay Foundation, please contact:

Hay House, Inc.
P.O. Box 5100
Carlsbad, CA 92018-5100

(760) 431-7695 or (800) 654-5126
(760) 431-6948 (fax) or (800) 650-5115 (fax)
www.hayhouse.com® • www.hayfoundation.org

Published and distributed in Australia by: Hay House Australia Pty. Ltd., 18/36 Ralph St., Alexandria NSW 2015 • *Phone:* 612-9669-4299 *Fax:* 612-9669-4144 • www.hayhouse.com.au

Published and distributed in the United Kingdom by: Hay House UK, Ltd., 292B Kensal Rd., London W10 5BE • *Phone:* 44-20-8962-1230 • *Fax:* 44-20-8962-1239 • www.hayhouse.co.uk

Published and distributed in the Republic of South Africa by: Hay House SA (Pty), Ltd., P.O. Box 990, Witkoppen 2068 • *Phone/Fax:* 27-11-467-8904 • orders@psdprom.co.za • www.hayhouse.co.za

Published in India by: Hay House Publishers India, Muskaan Complex, Plot No. 3, B-2, Vasant Kunj, New Delhi 110 070 • *Phone:* 91-11-4176-1620 • *Fax:* 91-11-4176-1630 • www.hayhouse.co.in

Distributed in Canada by: Raincoast, 9050 Shaughnessy St., Vancouver, B.C. V6P 6E5 • *Phone:* (604) 323-7100 *Fax:* (604) 323-2600 • www.raincoast.com

Tune in to **HayHouseRadio.com**® for the best in inspirational talk radio featuring top Hay House authors! And, sign up via the Hay House USA Website·to receive the Hay House online newsletter and stay informed about what's going on with your favorite authors. You'll receive bimonthly announcements about Discounts and Offers, Special Events, Product Highlights, Free Excerpts, Giveaways, and more!
www.hayhouse.com®